THOSE HAPPY MOMENTS

How a One-Year Experiment Led to Lasting Happiness

By Joëlle Marti

Those Happy Moments

© Copyright 2017 by Joëlle Marti

Please visit www.ThoseHappyMoments.com for contact details.

Cover design by Laura Penwell

Paperback ISBN 978-0-9997375-0-7
eBook ISBN 978-0-9997375-1-4

This book is dedicated to anyone who thinks they might like to be just a little bit happier.

And to the memory of my dear friend Joy, whose spirit, courage, and sense of adventure will always live on for those of us lucky to have known her and loved her.

Her very name made her the definition of the many Happy Moments she left behind.

Contents

How It All Started

In retrospect, it all started with a simple question: Why am I not happy?

It seemed silly, at the time. My life wasn't exactly miserable, and on paper, things were going pretty well. I had a decent job. I was in good health. I was still young-ish. I had plenty of friends. And I'd moved to London – a city I'd always wanted to live in – less than six months earlier. I traveled a lot, for both work and play. I had enough money coming in. So overall, things were fine.

But then what was missing? Where was that elusive "happy" sentiment that I felt certain I somehow should have been feeling? Why did I instead feel like I was carrying a weight around, all the time, which I couldn't really define?

I tried to answer these questions in many other ways over previous years. I'd seen therapists. I'd read books, watched documentaries, and listened to podcasts on happiness and manifesting good things into my life. I'd journaled religiously to understand myself better, only to get frustrated when I'd reread the sadness and boredom that regularly poured out of me. I'd gone back to school for an MBA, thinking surely that'd validate me – only to end up unemployed for well over a year and in substantial debt. Then I'd gotten over a bad relationship, finally found a job, and built myself a new life in a great new city. And I'd tried lots of other things, too: I'd seen a life coach for over a year, completing homework assignments for him like working on a vision board, taking dance classes, and writing gratitude lists. I'd even tried holistic approaches: acupuncture, meditation, astrology, and more. Honestly, I was pretty open to trying anything that might help me get out of what I felt sure was a rut of some sort. The biggest problem of all was: That rut was a constant. That rut was my life.

Across those same years, I'd confessed and cried in so many appointments and consultations and chats with friends and even private moments alone in the bathroom, and every single time that happened, I thought: "This is it! – that was the breakthrough I needed, and now I know what I need to do, and now things are going to change!"

...Except they never did. No matter what external changes I tried to make in my life, nothing truly changed how I really felt on the inside.

Note that I wasn't completely miserable. I wasn't struggling to get out of bed in the morning, and I wasn't seriously depressed. I just had this constant feeling of,

"Really? *This* is all there is?" It just didn't seem to matter very much. Life felt...small.

Which brings us to January 1st, 2016. And as I sat there, reflecting on all my cliché New Year's Resolutions of years past, and thinking about whether I'd write a depressingly-similar list to the year before, I just wanted to give myself a kick in the pants to do *something* that year. Something creative. Something a little different. Something that was just for me, but where I'd still be held somewhat accountable for actually doing it. Something that – forgive the morbidity – was about more than just paying the bills or simply going through life and eventually waiting to die.

So I did what pretty much any quasi-but-not-quite-Millennial would have done: I started a blog. I didn't even know how to start a blog, but there you have it. I called it ThoseHappyMoments.com. And on that first day, in my first entry on January 1st, I wrote: "Along the way, I hope to tackle the concepts of guilt and fear, open myself up to others, make new friends, and define a new kind of 'happy.'" I signed the entry, "Love, Joëlle" to acknowledge how personal it felt. And I hit publish. And then the next day, January 2nd, I came back for more. And again, the day after that.

And eventually – despite the vagueness of my original not-so-planned plan, my little blog experiment developed, day by day. Literally. I ended up writing 366 entries in 2016 – one for every day of the year, each one signed "Love, Joëlle" and personally valuable for what it was. Every single day, I explored a Happy Moment. Sometimes it was a "big" Happy Moment (a first date with a handsome new guy, becoming an aunt for the second time, being the only non-Indian at a three-day Indian wedding in Mumbai). Sometimes it was a "small" Happy Moment (a well-intentioned attempt at planting tomatoes, teaching my 90-something grandparents about selfies, watching *Sharknado 4*). Sometimes it was a happy memory from times past, and sometimes it was a reminder of how far I'd come.

The vague idea I started with was this: Even on a "bad" day, or a boring day, or even just a "blah" day, surely there'd always be *something* happy that had happened to me at some point in those 24 hours. And maybe if that was the moment I focused on from an otherwise not-so-happy day, maybe that's how I'd remember the day itself. And maybe if I collected enough of those Happy Moments – real, true moments that actually happened in my everyday life – maybe I could start to think of my overall life as a happy one, and to think of myself as a happy person—something I'd never, ever thought of myself as before.

And why a blog? Well, it kept me accountable in the context of my experiment. Again, not so much to other people, but to myself and to my future self. There was a limit, a timestamp, and a deadline: No matter where I was in the world that day, I had until midnight to find something happy about that day. Neither a shaky Internet connection, nor a lack of inspiration would ever stop me. I made a promise. And if I didn't keep that promise – even for just one day – the Internet-and-by-extension-the-whole-wide-world would know about it.

It was only later that I realized just how truly unhappy I'd been before I started the blog. Again, not because I was depressed or miserably, exactly, but because – if I'm honest – life was just getting away from me. I was turning 35 that year, and was nowhere near where I thought I'd be at that age. I was about as single as one can be; my corporate job was terribly misaligned with my own interests and values; I wasn't taking very good care of myself; I was hard on myself about everything; and I was unsure how to change things or whether I even deserved better. I felt like I'd tried everything to fix how things were, and nothing had really helped.

But what I noticed in writing my blog, one day at a time, was that the further I got into the year, the more I started to care about those Happy Moments of mine. Not because my blog developed a huge following, but because

I was being forced – sometimes against my very will – to notice the happy things in my life. That time my toenail polish matched London's red double-decker buses perfectly. The deceptive simplicity of making my first-ever batch of mashed potatoes. That day YouTube played me the ClearBlue Digital pregnancy test commercial so many times, I almost put my head through a wall (ok, so some moments were happier than others).

And even more importantly, forcing myself to notice Happy Moments every single day meant that some days, I had to create them myself. Just to have something to write about that day, or even on a whole series of days. That's how I came to challenge myself to certify as a yoga teacher that year. It's how I boldly pursued a cute guy I had a crush on – who happens to now be my live-in boyfriend; see, this stuff really works! It's why I tried black toothpaste, and glued glow-in-the-dark stars on my ceiling, and took a different route to work one day, and lost weight, and attempted to join the Alpine Sandwich Club ... you name it. I literally had to MAKE myself be happy at least once every single day – and somewhat amazingly, it worked! Suddenly, I didn't feel that niggling, weighty unhappy feeling all the time anymore.

What's In It For You

My lesson learned from this experience is, I believe, an important reminder for anyone: There is so much for us to be happy about. Countless studies have zeroed in on the psychological, social, and even physical benefits of keeping gratitude journals, and – based on my own experience and daily practice – I think the same principal can be applied to happiness. For every "My life sucks" moment, there can be a corresponding, "Hey, I'm not actually as unhappy as I think I am" moment.

Taking that idea one step further, consider the power of practice. Developing a small habit that is solely for you and your own self-care – as I did – can help you feel less stuck in those difficult moments and existential questions you may have been pondering. And it can also lead you to be more empowered to make other changes in your life.

Now, I'm not saying that everybody needs to start a daily blog to find his or her own Happy Moments. Far from it. For one thing, I left far too many a party that year at 11:45pm to whip up and publish a couple of quickie sentences. I promise, not everybody has to be a weirdo obsessive about it – maybe that's just me. We all develop habits differently, and it's important to find the one that works for you.

But as a starting point, I do think there is value in stopping and acknowledging that you, too (yes, you!) have Happy Moments – pretentious capitalization and all – in your life. Every day. Every single day. And it's worth finding the practice that works for you to celebrate them.

Try it. Write down – or say out loud - a few sentences, today, about what made you happy. Big or small, what was that something? It doesn't matter how silly you feel. Maybe today you got an email from a long-lost friend. Or maybe peanut butter M&Ms were on sale at the drugstore. Maybe your slippers were really comfortable. Maybe you had an unusually good hair day. Just do it. Then do it again tomorrow. Do it even if you're tired or sad or annoyed or angry. Do it because you don't want to forget that little moment from today where – however briefly – you smiled. You had that little inner spark. You felt something good. Distinguish this day from all of the others that risk bleeding together, and create a little corner of happiness through which it can be remembered as a *good* day.

One year after I started the blog on January 1st, 2016, I put it to the side. On January 1st, 2017, I wrote my last entry: a retrospective of the past year. I couldn't believe I'd actually done it. I wasn't even trying to do it when I started out, and yet there it was. I'd created a something. I'd created a whole year of memories, where – whenever I'd look back on them – I'd see only happiness. I'd see a whole year's worth of good days and silly moments and random happy stuff. Which made me feel great!

And what was even better was that the more distance I got from the blog, the more I realized that thanks to the habits I'd developed over time, the happy feeling continued. I was happier on the outside, yes: I was now in the best romantic relationship in my life, exploring exciting new career opportunities that felt much more authentic to me, taking better care of myself, and more. And most significantly of all, I was still noticing the little Happy Moments of everyday life – even if I wasn't blogging about them anymore.

And after about six months of that, I started thinking, "I wonder if there's more to this happiness thing?" Because maybe it didn't just have to be a one-year blog. Maybe some of the things I'd learned could help someone else. Maybe it was time to take that idea a little bit farther, and create another something.

And that's where this book comes in. It's a collection of some of my favorite blog entries from my year of Happy Moments, organized into 10 themed chapters. For example: overcoming adversity, challenging yourself to be happier, or – my personal favorite – finding the little totally-random Happy Moment you wouldn't have otherwise noticed. Each chapter has several entries, along with a retrospective "Tying Up Loose Ends" of what I learned from writing about that particular theme, and that I think could benefit you too.

At the end of each chapter is a series of short, workbook-style prompts to help you find some of your own Happy Moments. Use them and the examples scattered throughout this book as inspiration to find what works for you – or don't. Your Happy Moments are YOURS, so be authentic to yourself. And the more you do it, the easier it gets – and the more moments you'll have to look back on that will prove to you and your sometimes-stubborn self that it just can't be all that bad.

But do something. Promise yourself. Promise your future self. Heck, promise somebody else if you don't trust yourself. Don't go another week, month, or year coasting and worrying and guilting and envying and feeling sad. I promise you, no matter how stuck you feel right now, how unfocused, or even how scared ... you don't have to be as unhappy as you think you are. Life can be happier. Your Happy Moments are already there, screaming to be noticed, much as it turned out that mine were staring me in the face all along. As I wrote in that final blog entry:

"I think that's how a lot of things that end up being really personally important and special start out, when you think about it: Start with a vague idea, mix in a little spontaneity, stay committed and stubborn, and ... surprise yourself."

And, you guys, Happy Moments are *everywhere*.
They deserve to be noticed: Go out and find them.

Love,
Joëlle

So ... what now?

The 10 chapters in this book represent the 10 core themes I encountered when writing my yearlong blog. I've edited the entries in these chapters for length and clarity, and in some cases combined elements from several entries that tied together (the full, original blog can still be found at ThoseHappyMoments.com).

Some of these themes may resonate with you more than others, and that's perfectly fine. The chapters also do not have to be read in any particular order – chances are, like mine, your own Happy Moments are going to be a little all over the place.

I encourage you to use these examples as a sort of brainstorming exercise: can you relate to any of the situations or themes? What Happy Moment could you take note of, remember, or create in that type of a circumstance? If nothing comes to mind, that's absolutely fine. There were so many days I stared at a blank blogging screen for what felt like hours where nothing came to my mind either. I think what helps in those cases is simply to trust that the moments are there, and that if you just keep your eyes open for them, they're waiting to be discovered.

As you work your way through the book, I encourage you to jot down any thoughts, reflections, or Happy Moments of your own. Feel free to use the margins or spaces provided, grab a journal, or even start your own blog!

Chapter 1: WTF am I actually doing here?

Aka, the "Am I a weirdo?" chapter. Aka, the "But I don't wanna" chapter.

Throughout my year of searching for, noticing, and creating Happy Moments, I had many, many times where I wondered what all of this was for. At first glance, there was no intrinsic value to my blog project. It wasn't earning me money; it wasn't making me any new friends (at least, not at first); and it wasn't providing me with any sort of new revelations about the direction my life should be taking (at least, again, not at first).

And oh, there were some days where I wanted nothing to do with this. Days where I felt embarrassed, and stupid, and just wanted to quit all of it forever.

But somehow, as I kept plugging away day by day, I noticed that those "WTF" feelings grew less over time. I started to take some pride in my project, and, more importantly, to take some pride in myself. Even on days where I didn't have a lot to say, and really strained to find something to write about, I still proved to myself that I could do it. And that mattered to me. That was something valuable.

The first time I actually realized how much I cared about my new way of searching, noticing, and creating was on March 12th, almost two-and-a-half months after I'd started my project. I was at a party, having a wonderful time with a whole bunch of friends I hadn't seen in years. It was a blast. And yet I left about 20 minutes before midnight so I could run home and write a blog post about the experience. Yup, I was that girl. I picked a blog entry over a really great party.

And I asked myself that night: "Why?" It's not like I couldn't have just skipped one day, or even written an additional entry the next morning. No one would have actually cared, and at that point, early on in the year, I still hadn't even officially committed to writing every day. I just wanted to keep my daily happiness habit going as long as I could. And when I left the party that night, I knew that I *could* keep it going, and I *did* care. I think I'd had a previous tendency to lie to myself about how much certain things meant to me – it felt easier, somehow, if they weren't important. But this *was* important, and I was finally ok with admitting it to myself.

So what I learned over the course of the year was this: Even if you don't know WTF you're doing sometimes, or why you're doing it, what matters is that you *are* doing it. Actions outplay thoughts, intentions, and dreams. Every. Single. Time. That may sound controversial sometimes – i.e., "Surely dreams are *so* important!" – but it's true. Unless you work on the action piece, you'll never have anything to show for your dreams. For example, I've been dreaming of writing a book for many, many years, and yet until now, a dream was all it was. No matter how much you may want to accomplish something, how much you talk about it, seek encouragement to pursue it, visualize it, etc. – Until you can point to that thing that you actually *did* about it, it isn't a source of happiness. It's just a dream.

And I needed to wake up from quite a few dreams I was having and stop my life from passing me by.

My WTF blog entries evolved over the year, as did the Happy Moments that I noticed and created for myself. I actually found that the more the year progressed, the fewer WTF Moments I had, simply because I wasn't questioning myself and my dreams nearly as much anymore – I was just doing. And for those WTF Moments I did still have, I became more and more ok with them: more ok with not always having a great reason to find and write about them, and more ok with giving little nudges to my own life to make them happen myself.

Here are a few of my WTF entries, interspersed with updated side notes:

~~~~~

January 1ˢᵗ: Welcome to Those Happy Moments!

Welcome to a space where I explore the New Year in all its glory through what I'm calling Happy Moments. I am so excited to see what this year will bring. I'm that girl who likes to challenge myself with what comes next, who wants to lead a more meaningful and creative life from this day forth, and who still occasionally wonders what I want to do when I grow up (which, ahem, I sort of already am).

I'm also the girl who's finally decided to respectfully nudge my fears to the side while I actually try to do something about all of that. What will that mean? Well, off the top of my head the list of things I WANT to do in 2016 includes publishing my first novel, starting a blog (check!!!), developing my career with a focus in tech, growing my YouTube channel, finally learning to freakin' apply liquid eyeliner, and getting certified as a yoga teacher. Oh, and learning to do the splits. Will I accomplish all (or any) of these resolutions? There's only one way to find out.

Along the way I hope to tackle the concepts of guilt and fear, open up to myself and others, make new friends, and define a new kind of 'happy.' I look forward to the journey, and to the wild ride that comes along with it. Thanks for following along, and for creating your own happy and inspiring moments. We got this.

Love,

Joëlle

Side note: Spoiler alert – I accomplished two of the seven things in the entry's second paragraph during that year: starting the blog, and getting my yoga certification. That might not be considered a raging success, but I'll take it, largely because my priorities shifted during the year. For example, I no longer really want to work in tech, so that goal pretty much disappeared during the course of the year. For another thing, I accomplished lots of other things during the year that I'm equally or even more proud of.

Also, even beyond 2016, some of these are still on my radar. Publishing my novel hasn't happened yet, but you yourself are now holding evidence that I can publish a book! (And I'm pretty damn close to doing the splits.).

Finally, the point of these goals – and many other goals like them, particularly the kind set as New Year's-type resolutions – was to show myself the kind of person I wanted to be. I wanted to be the kind of person with a yoga certification and a YouTube channel. Not because that would make me a better person, but because I wanted to take some pride in my own accomplishments. Believe me, a full year of Happy Moments was the best thing I could have ever asked for in that respect.

~~~~~

February 18th: Just Keep Swimming

The past few nights, I have really struggled with topics to write about. The muse has gone missing, if you will.

And it's hard. It's hard to write a blog that doesn't have any sort of following, or even a totally-defined purpose yet. It's hard to put in that time every single day, when inspiration just won't strike and nothing in particular - good or bad - happened that day.

But gosh darn it, here I am. Keeping at it.

I read a short article the other day by Cammi Phan, a digital marketer and blogger, called "You Will Always Suck At What You Do, Until You Do This":[1]

Your first 100 blog posts will mostly suck. [...] Nobody can pick up a pen, then write and win a Pulitzer Prize right away. [...] The truth is no matter how smart you are. WE ALL SUCK IN THE BEGINNING. Most people give up right away. A few people stick around until they get it right. We suck and it is fine. Because it is just the beginning.

Now, I am not trying to win a Pulitzer Prize. I mean, I'm not saying I would turn one down exactly, but that's hardly a goal. But it is entirely comforting, I feel, to think that it does not matter in the slightest if tonight's blog post is any good. Nor if anyone else ever even reads it. If I just keep plugging away, something will take shape, and even if it never quite comes together in the way I expected, I've still created something in the meantime.

Sometimes, we need to just keep swimming...until we get to where we were supposed to, all along.

Love,

Joëlle

Side note: I still love that article, and the message it sends: It is ok to suck. If you try something, and you're terrible at it the first time? That's ok. It doesn't mean it isn't for you. It doesn't mean you won't get better. It doesn't mean you should stop doing it. If you like it, and your gut tells you there's some reason you're doing it, then stick around and keep plugging away at it. That's probably the most powerful way of tackling those WTF moments that come our way.

~~~~~

March 12th: About Last Night....

So the reason I find myself posting once again at just a few minutes before midnight is not EXACTLY my fault tonight. (**Side note:** This happened a lot. I suppose that's the point of deadlines, though—right?)

If anything, it's the fault of my MBA program, INSEAD, which had to go and organize a London reunion last night. Which dozens of not-even-living-in-London people showed up for, bringing our total count up to about 95 classmates, from all over the world. Many of whom I hadn't seen in the 2+ years since we graduated.

Which meant an amazing dinner at Beach Blanket Babylon in Shoreditch last night, followed by a brunch today, and finally a house party. We danced to 2013 songs, we sang, we hugged, we partied, and it was just amazing.

Sometimes I question myself on whether an MBA was worth it. The answer - for me - is unequivocally yes. Not because INSEAD was recently ranked the #1 program in the world, or because it allowed me the opportunity to live in new places and travel to even more. It's the people. It's the heart and soul. It's dancing until the wee hours of the night when you're really a morning person, and reminiscing about experiences you'll never forget, and laughing and smiling at alumni speeches that emphasize the importance of LIFE. Not just work. Not how much money we're making or what others are thinking about us. Not the bottom line of a balance sheet. Just life and being ourselves.

So much has happened since December 2013. Some of us have gotten married, or had children. We've almost all switched jobs or moved to new countries. But we're all still friends. And this weekend brought that all back. Feeling grateful.

Love,

Joëlle

Side note: Rereading entries like this one sometimes feels a little odd, because it's hard for me to tell if that is *really* how I felt at the time, or whether I was to some extent a little too conscious that I was putting my writings on the Internet. In this particular case, I think I do feel that the experience of my MBA was worth it, rather than the actual MBA itself ... and that continues to be food for thought.

What I have accepted, however, is the fact that I *did* do an MBA, and that I may as well be thankful for the experience at this point! Plus, when I wrote this, I was definitely on a friendship high. So I think I could have written absolutely anything at 11:55pm that night, and it would have counted for me as a Happy Moment. And I think sometimes that's the point: not what you're actually writing about, not WTF you were doing at that exact moment, but the recollection of how you felt at the time. That's making me happy thinking about even right now!

~~~~~

November 28th: Boring Days Count Too

Ohhhh, I'm having one of those days where I don't know what to write about. I've been staring at a blank screen for way too long.

My boyfriend just called and asked, "have you written your blog yet?"

(**Side note:** There is incredible value in letting other people know your goals. Other people can serve as external motivators and even guilt you into continuing to pursue those objectives. I know I personally needed that on a regular basis!)

"No...." I grumbled. "I don't know what to write about," I added, hoping he might have a suggestion. He didn't. It isn't his blog, after all.

I feel like I've already written about most of the things that happened today that I would normally write about. For example:

- *I let in my cleaner ("Lemons and Pine" – April 18th!)*

- *I walked to work ("Walk this Way" – February 11th!)*

- *I taught a yoga class at lunchtime ("Will Work for Yoga" – August 15th!)*
- *I went for gelato after work ("Everyone Loves Ice Cream" – May 10th!)*

And that makes me wonder - is it possible I've already written about everything there is for me to write about? Is my blog just starting to go around in circles?

But then I reminded myself that this is just one day, which might not have seemed remarkable in any particular way, but was still unique. And the fact that I'm still writing something today is one little step closer to a goal of mine, and that's worth celebrating in itself. Right?

Tomorrow I may have something more "momentous" to write about (...let's hope). But today is nothing to sniff at either.

Every day counts. Every step. Every Happy Moment.

Love,
Joëlle

Side note: I think it bears repeating that sometimes Happy Moments won't simply land in your lap. A lot of days *do* look alike, particularly if you have a "normal" everyday 9-to-5 job, or perhaps if you're a stay-at-home parent, or if you're going through a quieter time for some reason. It's so easy to go to bed at night and think to ourselves, *What did I actually DO today?*

And a lot of times, I think we're ok with that. But I wonder whether we should be. Because, sure, you can repeat the "same" day over and over 365 days in a row, but then what? The only thing different is that you'll be a year older. As bestselling author Robin Sharma says, "Don't live the same year 75 times and call it a life."[2] There actually *should* be something different and special about every single year, and every single day.

Rereading entries like this one is actually truly valuable to me, because – while I didn't at first glance remember writing it, almost a year later – the more I read through it, the more I thought, *Oh, yeah! That day DID happen!* And somehow, the very fact that I still took the time to notice a not-so-special day MADE it special. This is perhaps the best reason I can give for creating our own special, Happy Moments: They make those days matter. They bring just a little bit of extra happiness, attention, and meaning to days that otherwise would have gotten swept away entirely. Do we need to remember every single day in our entire lives off the top of our heads? No. But should there be something every day, just a little thing that we can take away from it and carry forward into a better, happier future? I believe yes.

~~~~~

Tying Up Loose Ends

Wrapping up this first chapter, there were so many more entries I could have selected to neatly fit into this WTF category. As I reread many of them, I was reminded of how much certain parts of my brain fought me on certain days. Thoughts came up over and over again, with little negative voices telling me: "This is stupid" ; "There's no point in this" ; "Nobody cares what you're doing" ; and the like.

And you know what? *Fuck* those voices. Who says you have to listen to such negativity, anyway? If you're anything like me, you probably have a constant stream of doubts and put-downs running through your head, and I'm telling you, *don't listen to them.*

If every writer or actor or painter or other type of creator had stopped creating at the first sign of criticism, we wouldn't have a single book or painting or sculpture in the world. If every baby stopped trying to walk the first time it fell over after a halting step, we'd all still be crawling around on our hands and knees. If every athlete quit his or her sport at the first sign of difficulty or minor injury, there'd be no need for the Olympics.

No, we don't all have to be actors or sculptors or professional athletes, but we should get better at recognizing those sneaky, cruel, lying little voices inside our heads that stop us from recognizing and rejoicing in potential Happy Moments. In a sense, we should all be "happiness athletes," exercising our happiness muscle, sticking to it, forming good habits, dusting ourselves off when we stumble, and keeping that countdown clock or finish line in mind. Because – happy or not – there is a finish line that each one of us will cross. After that, it's over. So anytime that "WTF?" question rears its head, and you can't think of a "good" reason why you're doing something, then the reminder of that finish line should be reason enough to either keep going or encourage you to change directions.

So each one of us really needs to decide, in a sense, *what kind of a performance am I going to put in?* And then we keep going. We notice the WTF moments, shrug at them, and do it anyway. Proving those voices wrong along the way. And enjoying the ride.

~~~~~

Prompt 1: WTF am I Actually Doing Here?

This first chapter prompt aims to bring a bit of clarity into why, exactly, a little additional happiness could benefit YOU.

What brought you here? Why notice your Happy Moments at all? What do you hope to take away from this? What actions could you take towards your dreams? What would your life look like if you were even just a little bit happier? Do some brainstorming now:

What do my own WTF moments / voices look and sound like? _____

_____

_____

How would it feel if I simply told those voices to fuck off? _____

_____

_____

When something good happens to me, I celebrate by _____

_____

_____

Something that helps me remember Happy Moments is _____

_____

_____

I'd like to be happier because _____

_____

_____

Chapter 2: What makes ME happy?

Aka the "What are my quirks?" chapter.

We've all got little individual quirks that help make us who we are, and that can prove to be a gold mine for happiness. For me, these were the days when I noticed the little somethings, those moments that made me smile and that probably wouldn't have made too many other people smile. Perhaps because I found something random to be funny, or because it reminded me of something. Or perhaps it was somehow linked to an inside joke of mine with someone else, or perhaps I instantly created some sort of inside joke with myself when that quirky little something happened.

And let's be honest: we really do all have these personal quirks, even if we aren't always very good at noticing them. We've all randomly smiled or burst out laughing in public (or wanted to, anyways), without really being able to explain to others why. We've all had those secret little moments where it seems like something exists just to brighten our own personal day. Think about it: What are some of your things – What makes YOU happy?

Personally, the answer to what made ME happy was a list that got a whole lot longer over the course of my Happy Moments year, though to be fair, I've probably always been fairly easy to amuse.

Just to give you a silly example, there are two words in the English language that I get an inordinate amount of pleasure out of saying out loud: "biscuit" and "saloon." I don't even know why – They're just both so fun to say! Seriously, try right now to say the word "saloon" without smiling. (Couldn't do it, could you?!)

I also have an absolute obsession with cheesy shark attack movies (as you're about to see). And weird songs that get stuck in my head. And if I could only eat two foods for the rest of my life, they would be chocolate and onions. And if that sounds to you like a horrible combination... yes, I'd probably eat them together. (If there were an *Onions & Chocolate* cookbook, I'd be first in line to buy it.)

But my broader point is that we all have these little things that make us *us*. And over the course of my personal happiness project, I embraced this more freely than ever before, and I'd encourage anyone to keep an eye out for their own little things and embrace them too.

Here are a few of my "What makes ME happy" entries – again, interspersed with present-day side notes:

~~~~~

January 7th: I Really, Really Love Bad Shark Movies

This isn't something I generally admit on a first meeting, but I really love shark movies. Low-quality shark movies, that fall solidly into the B-movie category. You know the type: bad special effects, nonsensical plot, generally starring D-list actors or washed-up TV stars from decades past. In other words: Jaws, *these ain't.*

To be clear: I don't avoid the admission because I'm embarrassed by this. My sister (a fellow diehard fan) and I have had intensely serious conversations about the topic in many a crowded room. Rather, it's to spare everyone else my launching into a crazy-long monologue about my favorite films, scenes, or the fact that, actually, Brooke Hogan's acting in Two-Headed Shark Attack *wasn't half bad. Whenever I do start babbling, I'm usually met by a nervous laughter, or a defiant challenge that "You're making those up."*

Am I, though?

Sharktopus.

Sand Sharks.

Jersey Shore Shark Attack.

As well as the slightly-higher budget options like Deep Blue Sea *and* Bait.

Mic. Drop.

31

And then there's my absolute all-time favorite, the classic 2002 masterpiece, Shark Attack 3: Megalodon. *I encourage you to watch the trailer sometime: That scene at the end? That is a man, jet-skiing straight into a giant shark's mouth.*

In Mega Shark vs. Giant Octopus, *a shark jumps 30,000 feet to bring down an airplane.*

In Sharknado 3: Oh Hell No!, *there is a scene where Ian Ziering and his father, David Hasselhoff, go into outer space to destroy tornadoes full of sharks with tanks full of rocket fuel because of course they do.*

I'm not sure why I love these movies so much. Escapist fun can be found in many other ways, and no, they're not the only movies I watch. I've tried similar genres--spiders, crocodiles, piranhas--but...I don't know, Lavalantula *just wasn't the same without sharks, even with fire-breathing giant arachnids. I guess I just like embracing my own silly little idiosyncrasies, the way we all do (right?).*

Excuse me--I'm being told there is in fact a heretofore-unknown-to-me film called Three-Headed Shark Attack. *This makes me so happy.*

Because if they keep making movies like this, then it means I'm not alone.

Love,

Joëlle

Side note: This wouldn't even be the only time that year where my Happy Moment of the day involved shark movies. On October 16th, I'd write about the experience of watching *Sharknado: The 4th Awakens*, which I enjoyed, but not overly so. Essentially I wasn't sure the science in the movie held up. Yes, I do sometimes consider scientific accuracy in my opinions of these movies.

Because, I mean, if a real sharknado ever hits, I want to actually have useful information to bring to the table. I sincerely believe that sitting through all four *Sharknado* movies entitles me to that.

Also, since writing this blog entry, I have actually had a few friends come up to me and say they enjoy shark movies too. I honestly feel it's brought our friendships closer together!

~~~~~

February 10th: Baaaaaaaad Horse

You know how sometimes a song can get stuck in your head for an entire day and just refuse to leave? Today was one of those days for me.

Not just any song, mind you. "Bad Horse Chorus," a 35-second jingle from the first act of Dr. Horrible's Sing-Along Blog.

What, you may ask, is DHSAB? Why, it's a 2008 three-part musical miniseries! Written and directed by Joss Whedon, of earlier Buffy the Vampire Slayer *(and, later,* Avengers*) fame! Starring Neil Patrick Harris (!) as the titular aspiring supervillain and (my favorite!) Nathan Fillion as the heroic Captain Hammer!*

It was written during the 2007-2008 Writers Guild of America strike, intended as a fun and inexpensive project to circumvent the strike conditions. It's been universally praised, won awards, and - ahem - has made me cry.

But...why today, exactly? I don't actually think I've even seen the miniseries since about 2009 (The whole thing is available on YouTube - thank me later!) Why did "Bad Horse" come galloping into my head of its own accord?

A bit of background: Dr. Horrible has applied to the Evil League of Evil, ruled with an iron hoof by the legendary Bad Horse. The doctor's quasi-sidekick, Moist, brings in his (slightly dampened) mail, which includes a response to the application. As Dr. Horrible opens the letter, three cowboys appear in the background and burst into song.

Does Dr. Horrible eventually make it into the league? Does Bad Horse vote 'yay' or 'neigh'? (see what they did there?) Does Dr. Horrible find love?

You'll have to watch to find out. Seriously, it's worth it. In the meantime, you can leave me to the lyrics that have trotted (get it?) through my head approximately 560 times today (which is the number of times 35 seconds fits into the 16 hours since I woke up).

I'm starting to get used to them.

Love,

Joëlle

Side note: My original blog post had the YouTube video for the song embedded, which probably made the entry slightly more cohesive. But that wouldn't have been the point, really. Again, the point of the 'What makes ME happy?' days was to help me figure out just that. Some days I *needed* a silly song that could make me smile 560 times in a row to help me get through yet another day at work. It was important to start noticing that.

And then, the next time I was having a rough day, or needing just a little bit of happy distraction – even just within my own mind – I could call up that song again. Or a different song. Or a particularly stupid scene from a shark movie. Or whisper the word "saloon" to myself, just to crack a smile. You get the idea. It was about getting to know the little positive parts of my mind, the ones I didn't necessarily show off – or even need to show off –

to the general public, because they were just for *me*, and they were there when I needed them.

~~~~~

June 12th: YouTube Really Wants me to Get Pregnant

You know those annoying ads that often show before the video you're trying to play on YouTube?

Recently, I have been getting one for Clearblue Digital a lot. I beg of you, don't go searching for it online. Don't encourage them. Allow me instead to describe it: Babies. Babbling. To the tune of 'Baa Baa Black Sheep.' Followed by an adult voice telling me about the best way to maximize my chances of getting pregnant, which essentially boils down to: "Blablabla. And also? Buy our product."

When I say I've been getting that commercial a lot, I mean every single day. And I am mystified as to why. I do understand why it would select me in the first place: quite simply because I'm a woman in my mid-thirties. Which is to say, many women of my age may indeed be looking for ways to get pregnant.

*But **I'm** not. And I feel like YouTube should know this! I haven't recently gotten married or engaged. I haven't looked at other videos involving babies. I haven't Googled one single thing that's even vaguely related to* *trying to get pregnant. I haven't shopped for baby clothes or visited any pregnancy blogs or even just once clicked on that looming "Tell Me More" link in the upper left-hand corner of the screen.*

Ring the changes a bit, YouTube! It's not all about gender and age! Couldn't you at least show me some ads about where to find a boyfriend, maybe, before trying to thrust me into single motherhood?

So today, you guessed it, I got the ad. I sat through it, painfully, for 20 whole seconds. And then I got on with my life.

Look, YouTube, I love kids. I may well end up having some. But not today. So please, take the hint and bring back the commercial about cats with thumbs. I love that one.

Love,

Joëlle

Side note: I still get that Clearblue Digital commercial. It still drives me crazy. And reading this entry, one could – quite fairly – wonder how this qualified as a Happy Moment at all since I sound so annoyed. But hey, again, it's a little thing in my day that, for better or worse, makes me roll my eyes, shrug, and smile. Sometimes I even get caught up and hum along to the tune.

Oh, and one last thing: now that I live in Germany, I sometimes get the same commercial dubbed in German, and THAT definitely makes me smile!

~~~~~

July 6th: Hans Schaudi, wo bist du?

I've recently developed a bit of a ... shall we say ... crush.

(Or rather, given the language involved, let's call it a "Krush.")

As such, and in order to impress said Krush, I occasionally attempt to break out a little bit of that sonorous, melodic native language of his, that is: German. Yes. German. Where there are 6 different ways to say "the," and oh yeah, don't forget to change the ending of every adjective depending on where it is in the sentence, and put the verb at the end, so as to keep suspense in every phrase!

Because I grew up in the French-speaking part of Switzerland, German was mandatory in school. I'll never forget the very first sentences I learned: "Guten Tag. Ich heisse Hans. Hans Schaudi."

Oh, the adventures of 13-year old Hans Schaudi, from our primary school German manual! His father,

Heinrich! His mother, Liesl! His dog, Lumpi! His totally-randomly-living-with-the-Schaudi-family-despite-not-being-related lady friend Lieselotte!

Hans and Lieselotte got up to all kinds of mischief while his father was off working at a bank, and his mother was at home, cleaning (...seriously. The Schaudis were not a progressive family. I'm pretty sure this manual was from the 1950s.) One time, they were walking through the forest hunting for mushrooms (...again, seriously), and Lieselotte tripped over a broken branch and broke her leg. She really was a bit useless like that. Hans fashioned her a splint and dragged her home.

There are certain phrases that have been burned into my brain for always and eternity because of that manual. "Schnitzel, prima!" because it was Hans' favorite. Or "Lieselotte ist nicht meine Tochter," Heinrich declared, emphatically wagging a finger to deny paternity. "Mein Vater und meine Mutter sind in Amerika" Lieselotte told us, attempting to explain her child abandonment.

I will never ever forget the word for necklace ("Kette"), simply because that's what Hans bought his mother for Christmas one year. Even at the time, I remember thinking Hans was doing all right for himself if he was buying his mother pearl necklaces before his 14th birthday. Oh, Hans. Memories of childhood.

Anyway, today, I rather proudly threw together a sentence for aforementioned German Krush, which I think is right up there with "Kommst du oft hierher?" ("Do you come here often?") or "Kaffee? Tee? Mich?" ("Coffee? Tea? Me?")

It was, "Meine Sicht ist vielleicht limitiert, aber blind bin ich nicht."

That means, "My eyesight may be limited, but I'm not blind." I'll leave you to imagine the context.

... And if nothing ever works out with Krush, there's always Hans.

Alles Liebe,

Joëlle

Side note: That German Krush of mine? His name is Steffen, and while it took a few more months, he eventually became my boyfriend, and now we live together. I'm pretty sure I can tie this all back to my romantic German pickup lines, which surely impressed him.

In all seriousness, though, this is a great example for me of taking something a little quirky that already amused me a great deal – in this case, Hans Schaudi – and basically taking that spirit or essence or whatever you want to call it a little bit further, in order to leverage a little more happiness. Remembering something that ridiculous honestly did put me in a happier mood to take

40

a little bit of a chance with someone I wanted to get to know better. You just never know where your little quirks might take you, if you pay attention to them and occasionally follow their lead.

Oh, and the joke's on me now, because now I live in Germany, and I *have* to improve my German!

~~~~~

July 27th: I Am Being Stalked

I'm sitting in the office on a gray, rainy London day, and I am being stalked.

I know this, because there is a very large, very disgruntled pigeon sitting on the wall right outside my window, staring at me. He's been there at least ten minutes.

I don't like pigeons.

In fact, I'd take it one step further than that and say that I actually have a slight PHOBIA of pigeons. Whenever people ask me, "what are you afraid of?", pigeons are the first thing that spring to mind. Not drowning or snakes or tight spaces or heights. Pigeons.

I have been told before that this is irrational and ridiculous.

"Like, you wouldn't cross the street to avoid a pigeon, would you?" a friend asked me once.

I narrowed my eyes at her: "It depends. How big is the pigeon, and is he there with his friends?"

But in my defense, pigeons don't like me either. I know this because they stalk me all the time. A few years ago, I rented a room for a few months, and I SWEAR, there were pigeons living in the crawlspace directly above my bed. They cooed and walked around all in the ceiling all the livelong day, except *whenever I'd call my roommate in to listen for them. They* knew. *They* wanted *me to look crazy. I nearly killed myself hanging out of the second-story window one day, trying to get eyes on that blasted crawlspace and whether it was possible to stop it up--to no avail.*

Or the time I innocently walked into Holland & Barrett on my lunch break - a health food store, mind you - and found a ginormous pigeon nesting in the bulk aisle on top of the honey roasted peanuts. I love honey roasted peanuts, and now they're ruined for me forevermore. I'm telling you, it knew that.

I may have to stay indoors today. So the pigeons can't get me.

Love,

Joëlle

Side note: Again, similar to the YouTube pregnancy commercial fiasco, this might not seem like the happiest of moments. But is it quirky and silly and ultimately ME? You bet. Do I get a lot of mileage out of this particular story, both with my friends and within my own head? Absolutely. Does it make me smile to think back on this particular moment? Like an idiot.

Oh, and do pigeons still follow me? Yup. Everywhere I go.

~~~~~

Tying Up Loose Ends

This is one of my favorite categories of Happy Moments, because they're the ones where you don't really have to do anything except notice the things around you that make you, personally, smile – regardless of what anyone else might think of them. It was with blog entries like these that I started to think, *Wow, I really can find reasons every single day to be happy.*

No matter our individual quirks, I bet we can each find something that gives us that little personal spark of joy – and faster than we think, too. I'm pretty sure if we all challenged each other to find one little thing in the next hour, we could do it. And I think that's a more valuable thing to be on the lookout for than running constant complaints or stressful thoughts through our heads.

What I found along the way with these types of "quirky" days was, I got to know myself better. I accepted myself more. I laughed with myself more – sometimes on the inside, sometimes giggling alone in the street like a maniac. It was my little secret as to why I felt happy in those moments. And that, too, made me happier.

I hope it can do the same for you too.

~~~~~

Prompt 2: What makes YOU happy?

Ok, let's focus on you now. This chapter prompt is all about honing in on what makes you YOU. How do YOU define "happy"? What makes you smile? What makes you tick? What might other people think is ridiculous, and yet you don't care and love it anyway? How could you honor that today?

Words, concepts, and ideas that I associate with happiness include _____

_____

_____

Some examples of things that make ME happy are

_____

_____

Quirks, experiences, things, hobbies, passions, etc. that I love *just because* and that other people might find odd include _____

_____

_____

Ways I could spend five minutes today honoring one (or more!) of those happy quirks are _____

_____

_____

Chapter 3: Those Pesky Adverse Setbacks

Aka the "But why meeeeeee?" chapter.

I'd be lying if I said that writing about daily Happy Moments for a year somehow made that year a super-easy one. There are always challenges to overcome, or difficult moments that come out of nowhere and basically blindside you.

Interestingly, the happier mindset I was striving for helped me look at moments like that differently – and even find the silver lining in them.

Probably the best example of that is when I tore my hamstring only nine days into the year. And I tore it doing something deeply stupid, by the way: I was trying to do the splits during a post-run stretch session. Oops. Anyway, it hurt like nobody's business, and I spent the first 48 hours wallowing in self-pity, much as I'd been prone to do for many of the prior setbacks in my life.

But then, two days after it happened, I decided to approach things differently. To joke about it, even. So I wrote a blog post called "Top Ten Best Things About

Tearing Your Hamstring." I had fun writing it. I even shared it with friends on Facebook, prompting one friend to respond, "Now *I* want a torn hamstring!"

The point was this: even "bad" situations don't have to be all bad. It really is what you make of them. Bad things can and will continue to happen to us here and there, and we can't always prevent them (although, fine, the torn hamstring thing was entirely my fault). But what we can control is our reaction to them. We can choose to move forward, shrugging it off in the context of life, and telling ourselves how grateful we are that things aren't worse. And yes, it's probably easy for me to say that when my injury wasn't a HUGE setback – but isn't that the point? We can't always predict how we'll react when a truly tragic situation comes about, but we can and should get a little perspective when things aren't really that bad.

Another way to consider those adverse moments is to take a much-needed backwards look at how far you've come. Frustrated with where you are right now? Ok, but where were you a month ago? Or a year ago? Chances are, you've made some progress and had some victories, right? Personally, I had a tendency to focus overwhelmingly on the negative aspects of my life, put myself down, diminish my accomplishments, and generally just deny myself happiness. Over the course of my Happy Moments year, that started to change. I became more forgiving and kind towards myself, mentally gave myself gold stars whenever I was proud of myself, and shifted my mindset entirely to say this: "You're DAMN RIGHT I deserve to be happy."

Close to halfway through that year, on June 5th, I was suddenly reminded of just how far I had in fact come since the prior year, and I wrote about that in an entry entitled "One Year Later." It was eye-opening to remember just how sad I'd been just one year ago, and how hard I'd been on myself for it. What an incredible difference to fast-forward to given where I was now!

Here are some of my top Happy Moments to tell the story of my progress over those pesky setbacks, once again with a little present-day context thrown in:

~~~~~

January 11th: Top Ten Best Things About Tearing Your Hamstring

In a nutshell: This past Saturday, after a long run, I tore my hamstring suddenly during a deep stretch. It was distinctly not fun. No more running, no more hiking, no more yoga--There go half of my New Year's resolutions. It is fortunately only a partial tear, and I fully intend to fully recover as quickly as possible.

In a much-bigger nutshell: 11 days ago, I started a blog called 'Those Happy Moments.' Not 'Those-Moments-That-Make-You-Want-To-Kick-Yourself-In-The-FACE-For-Pushing-Yourself-Too-Hard.' Which is why instead of whining, I have come up with....

THE TOP TEN BEST THINGS ABOUT TEARING YOUR HAMSTRING

1) With your leg elevated on a pillow, more opportunities to admire your new socks!

2) At last--a fine use for those ice packs you saved from your one and only Gousto delivery.

3) You may get to visit emergency care in a part of the city you'd never been to before. Tourism!

4) Internet research will surface numerous articles telling you that hamstring injuries are common in 'elite athletes.' You have a hamstring injury. Ergo, you are an elite athlete.

5) During your online research about such injuries, you will get shown anatomically-correct pictures of muscular posteriors and snigger to yourself.

6) You now have a bonafide reason to drop the word 'semimembranosus' into casual conversation.

7) 'Oh, you need help with that spreadsheet? Sorry, I can't. Torn hamstring, you know.'

8) Because, honestly? It could have been so much worse. Deep breath. Perspective.

9) You'll get to learn a little bit more about your own limits, and be more grateful for the fantastic health you enjoy 99% of the time.

10) Because even though it sucks right now, you KNOW that you are going to heal and be just as fast, just as strong, just as limber, and just as awesome as before, and that you'll have totally earned it, so THERE!

Love,

Joëlle

Side note: This is all so true, particularly the point about gratitude. I became MUCH more aware of and grateful for my body after this injury. Appreciating what you normally do have can go along way to providing perspective when something unfortunate happens.

My injury, by the way, didn't stop there. Throughout the year, I had several more setbacks. I had dozens of physical therapy appointments, and saw a half-dozen different doctors. I started running again, slowly and gently, about five weeks post-injury, but eventually re-aggravated the injury into tendonitis – right in the middle of my yoga teacher training. To this day, 18 months later, I still have occasional aches from it. But I can definitely appreciate how far I've come, particularly when re-visiting some of these entries!

~~~~~

February 13th: I Agree With Kanye West

Today was my first run in ages, five weeks post-hamstring injury. Watch me go! Watch me recover!

It's been a slow and frustrating recovery. A number of friends have told me, with huge smiles, "oh, you're healed!" when they see me walking normally. I wish that were true. I can still feel a twinge with every step I take, certain everyday moves are pretty painful, and I've got a full six inches of reach more on one side of my body than the other. I'm like the polar opposite of Gumby. I've lost noticeable muscle mass and fitness, and it's probably going to be another few months before I'm done with the pain and peskiness.

But anyway: happy thoughts! It was so exciting to take my running shoes down off the shelf. We get to go out and play!, *I heard them whisper excitedly. I dusted them off, laced them up, cranked up the Kanye ("That-that-that-that don't kill me, can only make me Stronger"[3]), and headed outside towards my beloved Regent's Canal.*

It wasn't actually fun. My thought process went something like this: Oh God, it's cold. I don't like this. Ow. Hamstrings are stupid. Great, now it's raining. *I had to take tinier-than-usual strides because I can't extend my left leg back as far as usual. I favored my right hip. I was a full 80 seconds-per-kilometer slower than I'm used to.*

But, much like Forrest Gump, I... was... RUNNING!!! And with every (tiny) stride, I felt just a little bit prouder. I wasn't making excuses—I was back astride the metaphorical horse that had thrown me, wearing purple riding boots and bright green jodhpurs. I made it to 5K, 2K longer than I'd set out for. And that felt pretty dang awesome.

I think Kanye is right (there's a sentence I never thought I'd type): sometimes we just kind of have to keep plugging away, through failures and injuries and tough times--they DO make us stronger. Those are the moments that shape us, and that we'll remember for the best in the long run. (Ha! Unintended pun.)

Hamstrings, you're on notice. It is ON.

Love,

Joëlle

Side note: Can I tell you? It's literally amazing reading this over again, reminding myself just how much I'd been set back. If I hadn't been writing about Happy Moments, I'm not sure I'd even remember just how limited my body became, temporarily. Looking back at it now from the other side of recovery, I'm just so incredibly

52

grateful that I could find the good – even in those more frustrating days.

~~~~~

May 12th: Hospital Gowns Are a Great Look

I had an MRI during my lunch break today.

Not for fun, mind you. It wasn't as if I just wanted to do something different, or I'd gotten bored of going to Prêt A Manger or something. This was entirely pre-arranged and to do with both my slow-slow-very-slow hamstring recovery. So nothing life-threatening or terribly serious.

So given that, I was sort of able to - dare I say it - enjoy *the experience. Insomuch as that's possible, I suppose, when you have to lie completely still in a confined space for 45 minutes.*

I mean, hospital gowns don't exactly flatter most people (myself included), but then again, you can't get a whole lot more comfortable than a flapping bathrobe and slippers, can you? Isn't there something sort of hilarious about wearing a garment that only comes in one size? Don't you sometimes wish more clothing were like that? (No? Just me?)

And another thing I loved was that you could choose music to listen to in the MRI machine. An actual MRI Music List! Bob Marley! 80s Hits! ABBA!

I opted for Adele. And when "Hello from the outsiiiiide" played, I was thinking that given my current claustrophobic location it would be better if it were "Hello from the inside" instead, and boy did I think that was hilarious in the moment. Oh, how I cracked myself up with that one.

In fact, I had some weird thoughts in that MRI machine. I thought about life, love, the mysteries of the universe, where I want my life to go, why I am who I am, how deep the depth of my thoughts was. And then at one point, I'm pretty sure I fell asleep. Whilst inside the world's loudest piece of machinery.

All this to say: I wish that MRI had been longer.
I had the perfect outfit and everything.
Love,
Joëlle

Side note: What actually came of that MRI was that diagnosis hamstring tendonitis, which meant I had to stop running *again,* and also take lots of care during all the yoga I was doing (since by then, I'd already started my yoga teacher training). The fortunate thing is that – in spite of the continued physical pain and frustration – I really didn't let it define my life. Instead, I embraced what I could do: I yoga-ed the Hell out of that teacher training, and I looked forward to my next run. And perhaps most importantly, I kept looking for unrelated good, happy experiences around me.

~~~~~

November 29th: Running Halfway There

This morning I ran just over 4 kilometers.

This is an entirely unremarkable distance, if not for the fact that it means my total runs since the beginning of 2016 crossed the 300km mark, or 50% of the 600km goal I had set for myself this year.

Now, obviously, it's the end of November already. In other words, I ain't hitting 600.

And in some ways that's pretty disappointing. When I set that goal, 600 wasn't even supposed to be ambitious. I mean, in 2015, I ran more than twice that: 1,352km. I'd only set such a low goal because I knew I wanted to focus my physical exploits this year more on yoga and other "softer" pursuits that would challenge me in a different way.

And then, in January, I got injured, and had to take a break from running. Then I started again in February, getting fairly aggressive a little too quickly, re-aggravated the injury, took another break, started again, and have been inching my way towards that seemingly-pitiful 50% ever since.

I am no longer "a runner." I don't have the muscles anymore, nor the breath control, nor the speed, nor the numbers to show for it. Sometimes that makes me really sad.

But I do have some things to show for it, don't I? I mean, I did (more or less) recover from my injury, didn't I? And I did prioritize yoga this year, which was my original goal all along! And like it or not, I did still run every step of those 300km, which is more than I ran in any year of my life before 2013 combined.

I'm sad I won't accomplish that goal I set for myself this time around. But I'm proud I kept going. Maybe some days that's all we can do: hold our heads high, put one foot in front of the other, and keep going.

Love,

Joëlle

Side note: I'm really proud of this entry – and happy to report that was the last time I wrote about my pesky hamstring that year! It's not to say it was healed entirely. But the point was—I didn't need to write about it anymore: I could simply let the healing take place, and focus on all the other wonderful things happening in my life. Besides, running 300km was nothing to sniff at.

Achieving goals is certainly wonderful and commendable. But let's not gravitate towards the concept of "failure" when things don't go as expected. The effort made along the way, and the happiness found in pursuit of such goals, are just as important – if not more so! If we play our cards right and maintain the right, positive attitude, they can even contribute to future goals we might not otherwise have considered.

~~~~~

June 5th: One Year Later

I think sometimes a Happy Moment can simply be defined as something that is clearly so much better than an UNhappy moment. For example....

One year ago tonight, I was at a really low point. Perhaps my lowest ever. It was the night I moved out of my ex-boyfriend's apartment after he'd broken up with me, and onto a friend's couch in San Francisco. I was suddenly single, homeless, broke, unemployed for well over a year, and I sobbed so hard that night I didn't actually even know my body could do that.

I'll spare you further gory details, but it's amazing now to think back to that night. Because in a year, it turns out a lot can happen! I got a job. I moved to London. I found an apartment. I reconnected with old friends. I made new friends. I traveled a lot, including to three countries I'd never visited before (Iceland, Malta, India). I'm halfway through certifying as a yoga teacher, I've drafted a novel, run well over 1,000km, and sooooo much more. All in all, that's not a bad year!

Is life perfect now? Of course not. Lots still to work on. I don't know where the next year will take me. I don't know if I'll stay in London, whether I'll start teaching yoga, whether I'll ever publish my book (it's coming, honestly!), or perhaps write another one. (**Side note:** turns out I wrote another one – *this* book – first!)

But when I look back at the period of June 5, 2015 - June 5, 2016 that's a pretty strong indicator of just what one year can mean. It's mostly been straight uphill in that time frame.

So just think where things could go in the next year. Exciting to think of the possibilities, isn't it!

Love,

Joëlle

Side note: What was perhaps most remarkable of all from that time period was how quickly things changed, and how convinced I became that there is a happy storyline our life *wants* to follow. Because here's how things went down: Before I got my London job, I'd been unemployed for eighteen months after getting my MBA. I got exactly zero job offers during that time, felt like I was falling into depression, and completely exhausted my savings. There were days I honestly thought it would never end. The only thing I was clinging to was my relationship, and then, when my boyfriend dumped me, I really didn't know what to do. It was honestly the lowest point I could have imagined.

But then guess what? I got a job – less than two weeks after the relationship ended. Almost as if that's what my life had been waiting for, in order to hand me an exciting new opportunity. And that new job took me from San Francisco to London and into a brand new life. Talk about one door needing to close for another one to open!

Oh, and by the way? While that job wasn't by any means my dream job, it did turn out to be where I met a *very* cute German colleague. And now - fast-forward again - we live together, and we're building all sorts of Happy Moments together left and right. So to recap: toxic relationship gone -> new opportunities -> happy new relationship. Sometimes I think life has a sense of humor!

~~~~~

Tying Up Loose Ends

I firmly believe that the key to addressing – and ultimately overcoming – adversity lies in perspective.

Now, again, I can't stress enough how grateful I am that my hamstring tear was the "worst" thing that happened to me all year. And I'm certainly not encouraging anyone to trivialize any truly difficult moments of grief or tragedy or heartbreak.

But I do hope all of us can keep that sense of perspective when we occasionally face a setback, a challenge, or even some sort of physical limitation. These experiences do not define us. They sit within a much, much broader context of what should be an overall happy life.

I feel there's tremendous value in looking back on landmarks like this – whether happy or unhappy ones. Sometimes just the act of looking back on a more difficult time can create a Happy Moment: thinking, "Wow, I'm doing a lot better now," and treating that as a victory. You know the expression about wearing scars as a badge of honor? Or, again, the Kanye West song about how "that-that don't kill me can only make me stronger"? How about, instead of being stronger, we strive to be *happier?*

I think that's always something worth striving for.

~~~~~

Prompt 3: Those Pesky Adverse Setbacks

What challenges or adverse situations have you faced? How did you react to them? How do you feel now when you look back on them? How might you take something away from those experiences?

Challenges I have faced include _____

_____

_____

Ways I reacted to those situations include _____

_____

_____

Examples of ways I could have reacted differently to those situations could be _____

_____

_____

Things I can learn or take away from past "bad" situations are _____

_____

_____

Chapter 4: Good Friends, Good Fun

Aka, the "See? I am awesome!" chapter.

During my year of Happy Moments, along with reflecting back on the bad or adverse times I'd been through, I also started to pay special attention to the good times I'd been through, particularly with the people I cared about. I had definitely been guilty in the past of taking those people – and the time I spent with them – for granted.

For example, my immediate family is very scattered: my Mom and brother live in different parts of the U.S., my father and sister live in Switzerland, and I lived in the UK at the time (and now Germany). Clearly, we don't spend a lot of time together, and unfortunately, we're pretty used to that at this point.

So as I developed a daily Happy Moments practice, I paid more attention to how lucky I am to have them. For example, for each of their birthdays, I devoted that day's post to them – even when my brother's birthday happened to fall on the same day I tore my hamstring. I also wrote about those few moments we did see each other during that year – the brunch with my Dad, the one day my Mom was able to come visit me in London, the time my sister and I strolled along the canals.

I wrote about time with great friends, too. My childhood friend Anna, whom I've been very close with for well over twenty years now. My High School friend Meredith, with whom I went on an adventure that year with a 3-day hike in the Scottish Highlands. My fabulous core group of girlfriends from the time I spent living in San Francisco. And many other friends as well.

I have at times felt like a very lonely person, and I sometimes − still, to this day - struggle with a bit of an "I'm not good enough for people to want to hang out with me" complex. But that said, writing about moments with family and friends did start to build a pretty strong evidence case against that complex. Because if that many wonderful people clearly did want to spend time with me, then surely that nasty recurring thought couldn't be true.

So for anyone else who's ever struggled with something similar − thinking you're not good enough, or you're not as smart or pretty or interesting, or whatever might be going through your head − I encourage you to start tearing down such negative and untrue thoughts with a healthy dose of reality check. Prove yourself wrong. Count your friends. Flash back on a fun conversation with a family member. Look back at old pictures of you smiling and laughing and having fun. Anything. Just don't blindly believe it anymore. Just because a thought keeps coming up over and over again doesn't make it true.

I encourage you to find your own ways of silencing those insecurities. Here are a few of the blog entries that made me smile, and that helped start to prove *my* little voices wrong:

~~~~~

March 2nd: Good Old-Fashioned Mail

Oftentimes as I'm walking home from work, I think about what I could blog about that day. What little special moments happened? What made me happy in some small or big way?

Today, the answer was waiting for me when I got home.

A card from an old friend, with a square of sea salt-topped San Francisco chocolate stuffed in the envelope for good measure. I love chocolate. And sea salt. And cards.

I can't even tell you how happy this made me. Not just because for once there was something in the letterbox that wasn't a bill or a reminder that I've not yet registered to vote. But also because it's just a real old-fashioned sign of friendship. As much as I love amazing tools like WhatsApp and Skype and Facebook that keep us all closer than we've ever been before - and that certainly make it easier on an expat like myself - there's just something about having a little physical memento that someone actually took the time to put pen to paper and create, just for me.

Today's lovely gift was from my even lovelier friend Liz, and I'm a little embarrassed that she beat me to it when I have been meaning to send HER a note for the longest time. She's a true friend, and someone I genuinely owe, big time. We went through some confusing times together over the past few years, and no matter how uncertain her own life was, she was always both my biggest fan and the kick-in-the-pants I often needed.

Then, last year, I went through an even tougher time where I sincerely felt like I was hitting rock bottom. And Liz literally took me into her home. For a whole month. For free. She listened to me. And made me homemade pasta in a real pasta machine and put on Netflix and bought me wine and ice cream because she knew it helped. (Remember the ice cream, Liz? Sooooo much ice cream.) And no matter how long I go without talking to her, or how many miles might separate me from her sunny San Francisco penthouse, I will never forget how it made me feel to have her there in those times when I felt most alone.

And I guess that's real friendship. It's not all contained in a card that traveled across the ocean, nor in opening up your home to someone in need, nor in a pint of Half-Baked Ben & Jerry's. It's just...there. It's a soul sister thing, the kind that makes you feel fuzzy when you hear a friend is doing great, or excited when something goes well for them, or giddy when you're looking forward to seeing them again and sharing a great chat and a hug.

I miss you too, Liz. Thank you, for everything.
Love,
Joëlle

Side note: It still boggles my mind that this happened, and that I was lucky enough to have a friend like Liz to take me in at one of the lowest points in my life. And Liz is a smart cookie – so if *she* likes me enough to do that, I've pretty much got to be a good person.

It's people and experiences like this who are worth remembering whenever you need to put a smile on your face, or even a little pick-me-up. Remember those friends you can spend time with without noticing how much time is actually passing, or where you can go a year without seeing them and it still feels like yesterday. I hope we've all got at least a few people like that in our lives – but chances are, we have more than we think!

~~~~~

July 30th: Sister Style

My little sister Dania is in London this weekend, because - jealousy alert - a friend with some pretty serious connections offered her a last-minute ticket to the opening night of Harry Potter and the Cursed Child. *See? Magic is REAL!*

I, however, am not in London this weekend. I caught an early flight this morning, and I'm currently sitting in Washington Dulles airport on a layover, on my way to my second (or is it third?) home of San Francisco! I haven't been there since I moved to London a little over a year ago, and I'm super excited.

But last night, my little (but taller) sister and I overlapped for just one evening. We took a nice, long walk along the canals, and grabbed a fancy dinner at what Dania referred to as a "chicos" waterside restaurant (Note: "chicos" in this instance refers to a slang expression for the French word "chic," rather than implying this was a restaurant that primarily catered to Spanish boys.) Then we headed home for a few more rounds of Heads Up! and a little bit of sister bonding time.

We could have used that little brother of ours in the mix, too. It's been a long time since the three of us got together.

But for one evening, it was nice to have my favorite sister all to myself.

Beat.

Even if she did go to the Harry Potter play without me.

Love,

Joëlle

Side note: In some ways, this evening with my sister was a nothing special kind of evening. In the sense that it was basically just dinner and chitchat, rather than a huge outing or celebration or anything like that.

But I'd argue that moments like these are even more worth remembering – particularly with people you care about and whom you don't get to see very often. Because then it's not really about the special experience on that particular occasion, but rather about the time together. Moments like these are what make a *relationship* special, not just an isolated outing once in a while. And relationships are what are worth cherishing.

~~~~~

November 27th: Friendsgiving and Cranberries

Yesterday evening was so fun - Friendsgiving! It's like Thanksgiving, with added friends!

After mashing up my first-ever batch of mashed potatoes, I made my way cross town to my friends' Kika and Rali's flat, and added my potatoes to the mix of food. All the traditional fixings were there: a full turkey, stuffing, gravy, sweet potatoes, casserole, and - my personal favorite - cranberries.

Cranberry filling is one of those things I kind of think just goes with everything. You can spread it on crackers, plop a dollop on top of a pie, or of course, swirl it with mashed potatoes. Soooo yummy!

As an American living abroad, I hadn't had most of these foods since last *Thanksgiving, and I was honestly really touched by the experience. I hope that next year I'll be able to celebrate the holiday in the U.S. with my family again, but in the meantime, this was truly special. It felt, dare I say it,* authentic. *Which is a weird thing to say when you're in London and you don't even eat turkey.*

After dinner, we sat around laughing, sang a spot of karaoke (new Thanksgiving tradition?), and drank some more wine. I didn't get home until the distinctly non-Thanksgiving time of 2:15am. Which meant today I was veeeeery tired.

But that's ok. It was all for a good cause: Good friends and cranberry sauce.

Love,

Joëlle

Side note: This was a lovely example – and rather à propos, as it were – of being thankful. There are probably plenty of moments in life where our automatic first choice isn't available – for instance, not being to spend Thanksgiving with your family. But in moments like those, ask yourself: what could be just as good? What might surprise you with how much fun you'll end up having?

Anytime something doesn't work out as we'd first planned, let's look for other options that could work just as well. Maybe you invite a friend out for a fun evening, and they can't make it? Well then, who else could you invite instead? Maybe you're not able to spend a family member's birthday with them, or attend a play they're starring in, or be with them on graduation day? What could you do instead? Could you call, or send a funny gift, or simply tell them you're proud of them?

Relationships with the people we care about are a huge source of happiness – no surprises there. So let's maximize the happiness we take away from them. Let's be thankful for having these people, near or far, in our lives. And let's notice the little moments together.

Because the more we derive from moments with others, the better we become at spending time with ourselves.

~~~~~

December 5th: Joyeux Anniversaire, Papa!

Today is my Papa's birthday, which gives me a great opportunity to reminisce about how lucky I am.

In some ways, my Dad is a bit of an odd one. You don't meet a lot of dentists-turned-astrologers, after all. Not too many Dads go shopping with their daughters for pendulums. Or listen to them talk ad nauseum about boys and career woes and Life's Big Questions, etc.

From my Dad, I think I get my interest in people, in the Self, in tolerance of others who may be wildly different than I am. I think that was a great lesson to have early on. In fact, both of my parents taught me that, in different ways.

My Dad and I are both the eldest of three kids, with some of the classic traits that go along with that role: we're both relatively "serious" in many ways, perhaps occasionally a little socially awkward, but with a silly streak.

For example, for many, many years now, my Dad has been doing this thing where he will spontaneously sing a song about "Le Petit Oiseau" ("The Little Bird") and various things that rhyme with that, like the French words for bicycle, back, pot, and funny. It's not an actual song, mind you: it's just something that came to him, and that he never, ever got rid of. It's a long-standing joke with my siblings about where that even came from, and I wonder sometimes if when I'm older I'll pick up a similarly ridiculous habit (my money's on yes).

Beyond the silly stories and good conversations, every little girl probably grows up thinking she has the Best Daddy in the World, but how many 35-year olds still think that? I think that's what makes me especially lucky.

Joyeux anniversaire, Papa.
Bisous,
Joëlle

Side note: Regardless of what our childhood looked like, I hope most of us can take away a lot of value from where we've come. What experiences and people shaped us? How are we like them? What did we learn?

And maybe, once in a while, it's worth thanking the people who helped shape us into who we are: parents, elders, friends, whomever.

It certainly can't hurt.

~~~~~

December 16th: Happy Birthday, Mommy!

Today is my Mom's birthday, and - since she'll love me for saying this - she's turning 29.

If there's one great thing my Mom and I have in common, it's a love of travel, and I'm super grateful to have gotten that from her. Both of us are all about making the most of this big wide world and the associated feeling of oh, the places you'll go!

It's especially impressive to me when I consider that, unlike me, my Mom wasn't born to travel. She grew up in different parts of the U.S., but never left the country until she was in college. In fact, I'm not sure she'd even been on a plane before then. So it was kind of a big deal when - as a single 19-year-old woman in the early 1970s - she picked up and moved herself to Switzerland to study French. It just wasn't the type of things you hear about women from small-town America doing back then (or, come to think of it, now).

She stayed in Switzerland for 24 years. In that time, she had three kids and started teaching us what was out there in this crazy world. Starting young. My own first-ever trip was at the age of about two weeks, to Fontainebleau, France — funnily enough, a little town I would study in myself more than 30 years later.

When she returned to the U.S. as a single Mom in the mid-90s, it wasn't easy. But she still found ways to treat us to some pretty sweet vacations. For my High School graduation, it was Hawaii. For my college graduation, Australia and New Zealand.

I'm especially proud that in her late 50s (oh oops, have I said too much?), she even founded her own travel company, We Wander Women, leading small groups of mostly-American, mostly-female travelers on affordable custom-designed trips. I'd like to hope that in addition to a love for travel, perhaps I got just a little bit of her independent/entrepreneurial streak, too.

Thanks for that, Mom. Happy birthday!

Love,

Joëlle

Side note: One of my favorite memories I have with my Mom was the time we went hiking and hunting for natural arches near Aztec, New Mexico. It wasn't one of our fancy trips – it's less than an hour from where she lives, it's not a huge tourist destination, and it was kind of rough going. I don't think even the other members of our family would have appreciated it all that much. But it was lots of fun, and it was exactly the type of excursion we both enjoy, and could enjoy together.

So sometimes it's useful to remember that one quirk you and someone else may have in common, something you can share once in a while, and maybe even organize together!

~~~~~

Tying Up Loose Ends

So how's that for a confidence booster? Spending time with family and friends, or even just hearing from them, or even just thinking of them, has tremendous potential to bring additional happiness to our everyday lives. And while it wouldn't take a rocket scientist to come up with that particular conclusion, I do think it bears repeating, especially for the many of us who have long struggled with self-esteem.

You don't have to have a million friends—I certainly don't. You don't have to be in a romantic relationship—I was stone-cold single for my entire twenties, and for most of my year of Happy Moments. You don't have to come from a huge family. But just flash back to those moments you've had together, when you made someone else smile, or when they made you smile, or when you laughed together. And when special occasions do come around – birthdays, holidays, etc. – celebrate those in spirit, even if you can't actually be with that special person.

As it turns out, it became much easier to be a friend to myself once I reminded myself that other people already wanted to be my friend. And once I started feeling a lot friendlier towards myself, loving myself became a more approachable notion. And that, in turn, attracted more great people and experiences into my life.

And that, ultimately, made me happier.

I hope it can do the same for you too.

~~~~~

Prompt 4: Good Friends, Good Fun

This is all about proving to yourself that you've already had plenty of good times with plenty of good people who like you, or who love you, or at the very least who enjoy your company. Don't skimp here – scribble all over the margins if necessary!

People in my life who enjoy spending time with me (or who call me, or text me, or tag me on Facebook, or have a nickname for me, or are pleased to see me when it's been a while) include _____

_____

_____

Some examples of good times I've had with some of those people are _____

_____

_____

Affirmative statement about what an awesome person I am, based on so many great people wanting to be in my life and good times to remember: "_____

_____

_____."

Ways I could reach out and create another good time with at least one other person *today* are _____

_____

_____

Chapter 5: Where's My Next Adventure?

Aka the "How can I get my thrill on?" chapter.

Ohhhhh, I love adventures. I love thinking about them, planning them, going on them, documenting them, and remembering them. They make me feel accomplished, bold, fun, and yes, happy.

Now, the term "adventure" probably doesn't mean the same thing to everyone. For me, it tends to tie back to travel. I've just always loved seeing new places and getting out of my usual comfort zone. But for some other people, perhaps you're more inclined to pursue your own kind of adventures closer to home. And you should! No one says you have to leave the country to have an adventure. Maybe it's getting on a mountain bike, or studying painting, or learning a new language, or starting a family, or launching a new business. Or even just walking around your own neighborhood and discovering something new.

But you know what I'm talking about, though, right? That tickle. That little rush of excitement when you think about it. That feeling of, "Ooooooh, maybe I COULD, and if I DID, wouldn't that be AMAZING!"

I'm pretty sure we all have our own version of adventures waiting to be taken on. Here are a few of mine:

~~~~~

January 16th: One Day in Venice...

What do you say at the end of a perfect day?

Late last night, I made an impromptu purchase of a round-trip train ticket from Milan to Venice. It's 2.5 hours each way, so I knew it would make for a long day trip. But I've never been before, and something told me that the one time I'd played blackjack at the Venetian hotel in Las Vegas probably wasn't quite the same. (I still love you, Vegas. Never change.)

I was up early on this beautiful Saturday, cruising through Milano Centrale station like a pro, taking my window seat, and watching the scenery go by, excited for the day ahead.

Upon arrival in Venice, I rather showed myself up by being so amazed at the watery scene before me that I missed a step and fell down the stairs of the station. I wish I were kidding. I'd been in Venice all of two minutes. Since I'm also still limping from last week's hamstring tomfoolery, I'm beginning to think I shouldn't be allowed to, you know, stand on my own.

Anyway, after I dusted myself off and haughtily ignored the open-mouthed stare of the nearest selfie-stick vendor, I grabbed a map to figure out which water bus would take me to the Piazza San Marco (it's the #2!), bought an all-day ticket for easy access, and I was off!

Since I only had nine hours to work with in Venice, I had to be selective. I'm fully aware that there are outstanding art museums and galleries all over the city, and sadly I didn't set foot inside a single one of them, preferring to enjoy the weather and the seemingly millions of walkways, alleys, and bridges (Venice apparently has 409 footbridges, and I definitely crossed a few dozen myself).

In my spur-of-the-moment research on Venice last night, I had come across pictures of an island I'd never heard of before: Burano. It's known for its brightly-coloured houses, which are painted like vibrant rainbows, where residents actually have to get permission from the government to approve the colours they want their homes to have. I had to see it for myself.

So from Piazza San Marco, I water bus-ed and hobbled my way to Fondamente Nove (and never has there been a better city to use GPS in--it would be SO easy to get lost in Venice!), caught the #12 ferry to Burano, and...words fail me. I absolutely flipped out at how surreally beautiful this place was. If Venice made my jaw drop, Burano took my breath away. I actually thought to myself, "from now on, all of my memories will be divided into 'pre-Burano' and 'post-Burano' moments." Just simply amazing. I'll never forget it.

I caught the ferry back to Venice at sunset (the witching hour!), and still had a few hours to grab some cicchetti, which are Venetian-style tapas. Tiny sandwiches, potatoes with onions, peppers breaded with cheese...mmmm. Then for more wandering, listening to singing gondoliers in the distance, and marveling at the amazing place I'm so glad I dragged myself out of bed at 6am on a Saturday for.

So I think the only thing I can say at the end of a perfect day is: Thank You.

Love,

Joëlle

Side note: I'm so happy to have memories like these, because it reminds me of just how fun it can be to travel solo. And again, you don't have to go far from home, or go for more than a day, or even just a couple of hours. Think about it: When you travel alone, you can do everything you want. No prearranged tour groups imposing activities on you; no friends/partners insisting on the things they want to see; just you, doing that thing you do. I'd encourage anyone to try it – what's the nearest day trip or other form of adventure you could try?

~~~~~

March 19th: Reminder: I Live in London

A realization has hit me this morning, as I was facing the prospect of a rather empty Saturday with nothing planned until the evening.

That realization is: I live in LONDON. London has things to do! Exciting things! Adventurous things! Quiet things! Loud things! Oh-so-many things! There's simply no excuse to not find something fun to do.

So I've spontaneously decided to get myself over to an attraction I've been curious about for several years: The Emirates Air Line. Not the actual airline, mind you: it's actually a cable car that crosses the River Thames from London to Greenwich in about 10 minutes. It goes over the O2 arena at a height of 90 meters (300 feet) above the river, so if I'm lucky, I'll get a great view of London!

It's a gray day, but no matter. There are adventures to be had. Once I'm on the other side, it looks like I'll be...well, pretty much in the middle of nowhere. But maybe I'll take a long walk to the heart of Greenwich, to the Royal Observatory, the National Maritime Museum, the Cutty Sark, or the little town itself. Maybe, maybe, maybe.

I don't know how long I'll end up living in London for, but I do know I don't want to leave with regrets.

Now, how do I actually get there?

Love,

Joëlle

~~~~~

Side note: Days like this were a great reminder to myself – always seize the day, because you don't know how long you'll have to do so. I ended up living in London for exactly two years, and I'm happy to say I left with no big regrets in terms of bucket list things I wanted to do.

Stop putting off the things you're interested in doing: just go on an adventure and do them!

~~~~~

April 10th: First Class on a Bus

You know one experience that's uniquely London?

Sitting in the front seat of the top deck of a bright red double-decker bus. This is by far the most coveted of all the bus seats, such that every time I score it, I feel as though I've done something to deserve it!

I imagine it as the equivalent of sitting in an airplane cockpit--albeit without the actual flying part. Still, for only £1.50, you get a pretty nice view. You can look down on people, shops, and the world below. You can look straight into second-story windows and observe people working and living. You can wave at fellow privileged top-deckers in oncoming buses. (They'll most likely ignore you, but hey, spread the love!)

Plus, the buses themselves are pretty iconic, which doesn't hurt.

It's just a little "Yay, London!" moment in my book. And that's always nice.

Love,

Joëlle

Side note: See? Lots of experiences to be found closer to home! Even a seemingly-mundane activity like riding a bus could be considered as an adventure with the right attitude. What could the equivalent be where you live? And how could you appreciate it just a little bit more the next time it happens to you?

~~~~~

April 21st: Saris and Spices, Here I Come!

I received a very welcome email last night from the good people in the Indian government.

"Application Status: Granted", it said.

"Hurray!", I said.

Let me back up: a few weeks ago, my good friend Ritesh casually mentioned to me that his cousin was getting married in Bombay, and that he'd be traveling home for the wedding.

"Ooooh, how nice! I've always wanted to go to an Indian wedding!" I exclaimed.

"You should come!" he responded.

Oh, sure, I thought to myself sarcastically. I'll just pack my bags and go all the way from London to India for only a couple of days, to attend the wedding of someone I've never met! Nothing unusual about that!

And then I thought about it. And looked at the calendar. And realized I've only taken one day off so far this year. And then I looked at plane tickets, and realized they weren't as expensive as I'd have expected. And then I imagined traveling to a country I've always wanted to see and never have, and my little "Yay, yay, yay!" light lit up inside.

The next thing you know, I was buying a sari blouse off eBay.

I know I'll only be scratching the surface of a country with many marvels and much magic.

But what better time to start?

Love,

Joëlle

Side Note: A few people told me I was crazy to travel to India for only six days, but look at what I was able to fit in: A three-day Indian wedding, a visit to the Taj Mahal, and a wild ride around Delhi. That's not even counting amazing food, lovely people, general culture, and just an awesome overall feeling. When you set your mind to it, you can really do so much when you travel, and it doesn't have to be as time-consuming or expensive as you fear. Let's seize the day! Get on a train, a plane, or even a bicycle. Go visit your nearest museum or art gallery. Stay curious! It's a big world out there.

~~~~~

August 20th: London Luck

I'm writing this on a train from London to Edinburgh, and while I'm crazy-excited to spend the next week exploring Scotland, I'm also feeling awfully lucky at the moment to live in London.

Last night after work I met up with my visiting friend Meredith and we went for a LONG walk. We started at the British Museum, walked through Covent Garden, down south and across the river to Southbank, towards Southwark, then back across the river to Westminster, Trafalgar Square, and finally ending in Covent Garden for a nice dinner. We saw sights like the

Houses of Parliament, Westminster Abbey, the London Eye, the Shard, the skyline of the City skyscrapers, West End theaters, and so much more.

It was a gorgeous, sunny evening, and as she kept commenting about how beautiful it all was, and what a great city London is, I found myself looking around and thinking, "Well....yeah!"

I think it's useful sometimes to see your city through the eyes of an openmouthed newbie. Maybe I should be appreciating London a bit more. Maybe it's become commonplace, or maybe I'm just too quick to think about the things that aren't exactly as I envisioned them being at this point in my life. I thought I'd have a bigger flat, and a car, and probably lots of other things too, but when I just look around at what I do have, and where I do live ... I'm really pretty insanely lucky.

And regardless of how long I actually end up living in London, I don't want to look back later in life and think that I didn't take advantage of it, or appreciate it in every way that it deserves.

You got me, London. I'm lucky to be here.

Love,

Joëlle

Side note: It's probably easy for some people to think, "Well, that's all very well and good when you live in a place like London, but what about if you just live in a small town with fewer adventures to be had?"

But I would argue that there are adventures to be found no matter where you live. In fact, living outside a big city often offers more of them! The point is that no matter where we live, and no matter for how long, and no matter whether it was even our choice to be there in the first place, we should always have a feeling of luck. Every place has something to offer, new things to try, and excitement to be had. Otherwise we're just not looking hard enough.

~~~~~

Tying Up Loose Ends

I'll be honest: This has been one of the hardest chapters to write, albeit also one of the most rewarding. It was hard in the sense that I had *so* many "adventures" to choose from in that one year, and I didn't want to just mindlessly turn this into some sort of travel guide. I really wanted to reflect on what those experiences have taught me, and showed me.

It was rewarding in the sense that it's really renewed my sense of how lucky I am – a great reminder for those days when those sneaky little voices in my head start telling me that isn't the case. Just reading about those "yay, yay, yay!" feelings I wrote about brings them back, and makes me feel happy. And it also makes me want more of them!

I can't encourage it strongly enough: Go on adventures of your own. Seek them out. They don't always have to be big, or far away, or crazy. Try to turn more mundane-seeming experiences into adventures. For instance: how could a trip to the supermarket become an adventure? Or a day at school? Or driving to work? Challenge yourself in your "normal" life, because I promise, if you can find adventures there, you'll find even more if and when you *do* go beyond your comfort zone.

So, where will *your* next adventure be?

~~~~~

Prompt 5: Where's My Next Adventure?

This is all about finding adventures – whatever that means to *you* – and creating them all around you. What are those "yay, yay, yay!" things that get you excited? Where would you like to go, and what would you like to do? What have you always been curious about in your own backyard, but haven't tried because you aren't a "tourist?" How could you turn something that at first glance might seem mundane into something exciting?

Things that provide that "tickle" of excitement for me include _____

_____

_____

The most adventurous thing that happened to me this week was (challenge yourself here!) _____

_____

_____

I'd like my next adventure to be _____

_____

_____

Something I've been curious about in my own neighborhood / town, but haven't tried yet, is _____

_____

_____

Copy the following statement (or another similarly-affirmative one of your choice, so long as it feels right): "I pledge to take myself on more adventures, whether near or far, daring or silly, unfamiliar or commonplace. I promise to honor the adventurous side of me, from this day forth." _____

_____

_____

Chapter 6: Challenging Yourself – Because Nobody Said This Was Easy

Aka the "I didn't know I could do that!" chapter.

One of the greatest things that came out of my year of Happy Moments was how much more willing I became to challenge myself. I'd always previously tended towards shyness and not-quite-daring to do the things that inspired me. How many times had I not pursued a hobby or interest, for fear that I wouldn't be good enough, or that others might not "get" it, or that I would fail? My intentions were always good, but I lacked the courage to follow through on them. I was constantly scared of failure, constantly insecure, constantly envious of others who were pursuing their interests, and constantly watching my life pass me by.

But after a few months of noticing and writing about Happy Moments, I started wanting to *create* them – big, fat, memorable Happy Moments. And that's where, bit by bit, the challenges started coming in.

And during that year, it was really one big overarching challenge that I ended up taking on: that of becoming a yoga teacher. It was something I'd been thinking about for years, but had never before taken the slightest step towards pursuing. And as it turned out, there were a whole bunch of smaller challenges wrapped into that one big one: signing up to the course in the first place, showing up, practicing every single day, passing my exams, and, eventually, teaching my first class. Every time I achieved one of those things, it renewed my sense of confidence in myself, helped me conquer just a little bit more fear, and – of course – provided me with yet another Happy Moment. So when something feels impossible, see if you can break that huge challenge down into bite-sized, approachable pieces. That proved incredibly valuable for me.

And since then, those experiences and their payoffs have made me much more willing to take on other challenges. Obviously, not everyone is going to become a yoga teacher (I mean, for one thing, there'd be way too much competition for me!), but I do hope that we each have a number of pursuits we can go after – in spite of any doubts or fears.

In my opinion, the missing piece of why I wasn't pursuing challenges earlier on (for instance, why I hadn't signed up for a yoga teacher training earlier) ties back to one of my favorite parables: That of jumping off a cliff.

Jumping off a cliff is typically seen as something crazy. "If XYZ jumped off a cliff, would you do that too?!" is something I remember being told as a child. The implication being: You'll get hurt! You're being stupid! It's way too scary! It's safe here, away from the edge! You could DIE!

But what we often fail to admit to ourselves is that big challenges or changes of direction in life are almost always scary and full of uncertainty. When we look at the people who are already doing the things we ourselves would like to do, we forget that they almost definitely had moments of fear and doubt too! But the difference is: They jumped.

And when you *do* jump, of course there is a chance that you might get bruised and scratched on the way down. Challenges, by definition, aren't supposed to be easy. So keep repeating to yourself: "At some point, a net will catch me."

You don't have to know what the net looks like yet, or how far down you'll be before it does catch you, or even if that first net will hold your weight. Just know this: If you keep putting in the work, something will catch you. Something *always* does. When I was involuntarily unemployed for 18 months, the only thing that kept me going some days and continuing in the job search was the knowledge that it would end eventually, simply because it *had* to. When I was sleeping on a friend's couch and totally heartbroken after being dumped, I knew it wouldn't last forever, simply because it *couldn't*. That certainty, and the efforts I continued to put in, eventually got me to a place where I could be dramatically happier: a job that changed my life in unexpected ways, a healthy new relationship, and so much more.

And it's the same principal with any challenge that is driven by something we *want* to achieve (or at least try out): *Things won't always be this scary.*

But you have to jump.

Spoiler alert: This chapter is a little different from the others in this book, because it tracks one big challenge start-to-finish, rather than diverse, unrelated entries like the other chapters. The point for me was to see how a huge challenge – one that had previously seemed unattainable to me – could in fact be broken down into elements that were much more approachable.

Here's how that particular leap of faith came about:

~~~~~

April 13th: Yogaliciousness and Musings

I've just gotten home from an informational session at YogaLondon, *a dedicated teacher training school.*

Yes, I'm thinking of training as a yoga teacher.

In some ways, it seems crazy: It's indulgent. It's expensive. My hamstring is still bothering me more than

three months after I tore it. I don't know if I'll have time.
I don't know if I'll be any good. I don't know if I'll like it.
I don't actually know if I want to be a yoga teacher. The
girl behind me had cuter yoga pants than I did. Maybe
this won't work out and then I'll just die poor and lonely.

In other words: excuses-excuses-excuses, with a
side of fear.

There were about 30 of us packed into a room in a
Tibetan Buddhist Center. We started with a 30-minute
introduction and posture analysis, where the teacher
demonstrated the foundations of a particular pose:
downward-facing dog. Spread your fingers wide, rotate
your triceps outward, spin your upper legs inward,
press your weight from your hands into your feet. And
so on. Then we did a quick practice with partners, trying
out a posture correction. This felt great--I've done a lot
of downward dogs, but to really take the time to figure
out all the little components was awesome.

Then we had a one-hour class, which felt terrific.
Though if I'm honest, a small part of me was keeping an
eye on other people in the room: Is she better than I am?
What about her? Should I even be here? *Hello, imposter*
syndrome, my old friend!

With that said, the larger *part of me was pretty*
damn happy to be there, challenging myself and
listening to an idea I'd been batting around off-and-on
for a few YEARS.

95

After the class, there was a useful Q&A, and then it was over. It was absolutely worth going. I don't know if I'm going to go through with it, or if so when and how, and it must be said my bank account wouldn't exactly thank me for it. So there's certainly plenty of reasons I can come up with not to do this.

But...if there's something you've been thinking about for a long time and wanting to explore, then...isn't that something worth listening to? Shouldn't that voice become louder than the excuses-excuses-excuses-and-fear voice?

Lots to think about as I fall asleep tonight.

Love,

Joëlle

Side note: I could have listed dozens more excuses not to take this course. Boy was I nervous about this – it's hard to explain just how much, but I remember times where I was literally shaking. Rereading this, I see so much fear talking. Obviously, it would have been *so* much easier to just not do it.

But I did it anyway. I jumped. I listened to that wanting-to-explore voice, which ultimately was louder than the excuses-and-fear voice. And I'm so glad I did.

~~~~~

April 25th: Yoga Teacher Training – Weekend One

Remember how 12 days ago when I went to a taster session for wannabe yoga teachers? Remember how I said I didn't know if I was going to go through with it?

Yeah, I signed up the next day.

It was a whim. They had a session starting the following week. It happened to have an open slot after someone dropped out. I shuffled my excuses-excuses-excuses (with a side of fear) off to the side. "Count me in," I said.

And thus, this past weekend I started my new yoga journey to who-knows-where. I'm taking the 200-hour course through YogaLondon. It's three weekends a month for three months, so if all goes well, I'll be a Registered Yoga Teacher by the end of July, which is a real title, which means that similar to PhDs, I can totally have business cards printed with "RYT" after my name (and yes, that's the first thing I thought of when I learned about the certification. Am I zen or what!)

(**Side note:** I didn't actually end up doing this. But the point is, I *could* have.)

So Friday nights from 6-9pm, and Saturdays and Sundays from 9am-6pm, I need to be present and accounted for, with my reading and homework done, ready to go. I've also committed to a six-days-a-week practice outside of class.

This first weekend was focused primarily on learning Sun Salutations A and B. We broke down every single pose, along with transitions. We learned adjustments, modifications, and progressions. We wrote scripts for ourselves. We had a lecture on different kinds of breath I'd never even heard of. It was exhausting.

And I realized that wow, I have a lot to learn. It's actually kind of incredible how much I'm supposedly going to know in just three months. I'm not going to lie: it feels really daunting. Saturday night I came home after the first full day and almost burst into tears because the magnitude of what I've signed up to do had just hit me.

(**Side note:** This was far from the only time I nearly or actually burst into tears during the journey. Tears are ok. They mean you care.)

In fact, if dropping out were an option at this point, I can't even swear I wouldn't do it. I have so much else going on already, and it's a scary new challenge-y thing. I don't always like scary new challenge-y things.

But I've committed, and I'm going to do my best, and that's really all anyone can ask of themselves, right? So let's see where this goes. Namaste.

Love,

Joëlle

Side note: While I wrote about every single training weekend, you'll likely be relieved to know I didn't include every yoga blog entry I wrote during the year in this book. But indeed, there was a lot more to be done besides just turning up for the weekend classes. What with working full-time, business travel, and all the other things I already had going on, I almost totally gave up on having a social life during those three months. But it was so, so worth it to me – and I think that, for most challenges that truly matter to us, we're ultimately willing to sacrifice more than we might initially think.

And I'm happy to say that this became a recurring theme throughout the duration of the program. Friends would routinely ask me, "When do you have any free time? Isn't it tough not having a real weekend anymore?"

And I'd honestly be able to answer that No, it *wasn't* tough, largely because what I was doing on the weekends was so much more interesting and enjoyable to me than what I was doing the other five days of the week. When you're doing something you truly care about, you simply find a way to make it work, no matter how busy or scared you are.

~~~~~

July 11th: Yoga Teacher Training – Weekend Nine

Yesterday night, I wrapped up the 9th weekend - out of 10 - of my yoga teacher training.

I've said this pretty much after every weekend, but I can't believe it. I really can't. This was such a whim when I signed up for it. I didn't know if I could do it, or if I would like it. And I don't like it. I LOVE it. I can't believe what it's done for my confidence, my self-respect, or for the way I look at my life. I'm simultaneously sad and happy that it's almost over.

As usual, it was an exhausting, yet wonderful, weekend. Friday evening we had a one-hour practice, followed by our first of three exams: anatomy. Ohhhh, anatomy. Not my forte. So how did it go? Well, I think I probably passed. I knew the bones and the muscles, and I kinda-sorta knew the postures to avoid for people with hypertension and hypotension and various injuries, and which muscle laterally flexes the spine and so forth. We shall see.

Saturday morning was my turn to be teacher's assistant during the two-hour morning practice. I taught a few poses to the whole group, and mostly wandered around the room doing adjustments. Adjustments are hard. You have to be careful not to hurt yourself or the student, not to throw anyone off balance, and to make sure your adjustment is actually helpful. You have to make split-second decisions: "Would this student benefit from an adjustment? If so, how can I best help them in the next five seconds?" Also, if you're adjusting a particular student on, say, the right side - and then five minutes later you teach the same pose on the left side, you should ideally remember to be there to adjust them again, rather than being way across the room helping someone else.

We had more business courses, more teaching practice one-on-one, a pub quiz style review of philosophy, a lecture on how to modify for pregnant women, and a discussion on how to market ourselves using social media. My head is FULL, but my heart is happy.

I honestly feel so sad about this journey coming to an end, even if I know another one will be beginning right behind it. I feel like I've found myself a little tribe of fellow yogis and friends, 19 other women I've learned from and cried with and laughed with, and that I'll miss when it's all over. I really feel genuinely lucky to have connected with such a wonderful group of people. I just don't know what else to say about the experience. It's been so special.

There is one weekend left. A philosophy exam, a practical exam, and a final day for graduation.

And then, we will jump out of the nest and fly.

Namaste.
Love,
Joëlle

Side note: There was so much that happened between weekends one and nine, and my enthusiasm for the course built up somewhat gradually. Every weekend in between, I let go of just a little bit more fear, until I got to the point where I could simply trust that everything was going to work out just fine.

Again, a sense of *knowing* is a powerful thing: Much as you can keep telling yourself that something difficult can't and won't last forever, you can also tell yourself that feelings of fear or nervousness will gradually dissipate. "Ok, I'm a little scared or uncertain right now, but I know I'll be less scared in the future if I just keep trying and learning."

It would have literally been impossible for me to not get better at teaching yoga after taking a 200-hour course and doing all that hard work – did that mean I was suddenly the best teacher ever, or that I couldn't still be nervous about it? Of course not. But I still developed a much better understanding of what I was doing, and I knew that I could only keep improving, given time and effort. That's how challenges work: if you actually take the leap and take them on, there's no way you won't get better at what you're trying to do.

~~~~~

July 23rd: Yoga School is Letting Out

Today, I passed my last yoga exam, meaning that tomorrow, after the ceremony, I'll officially be a certified yoga teacher.

I'm truly grateful. Unlike my frequent rambling blog posts, I'm actually kind of struggling to find the words. Today was just...great.

Our final exam was the practical, where we actually had to teach one of our fellow students a one-hour sequence. We were paired up, with three or four pairs teaching at once. The really fantastic thing is that every single one of us passed. There's been such a feeling of community in this class, and I'm so proud to have been a part of this group.

Today felt good. There's plenty left to learn, of course, but I had a real feeling of peace during my exam. I didn't feel nervous. All I felt was: let's do this. So we did. And it worked.

I have been thinking a lot lately about what yoga - and this class - has meant to me. Not yoga as in "poses that make you strong and flexible," but rather yoga, the thing that each of us has access to in some shape or form: effort towards stillness. That's it. For some, it's *hopping on the mat. For others, it's writing in a journal. Or taking a walk. Or sitting and staring out the window for a few quiet moments.*

What's your yoga?

Love,

Joëlle

Side note: Our teacher said something beautiful on the last day of our training, which has stuck with me ever since:

"Remember that every time your mind told you over the past three months, 'I can't do this,' it was wrong."

You can do hard things. You can take on challenges. You can get dramatically better at something in only a few weeks or months. You literally *can* do this, whatever 'this' means to you.

~~~~~

August 15th: Will Work for Yoga

At lunch today - *gulp!* - I taught my very first yoga class.

Not my first teacher-training-style class. Not my first friends and family class. My first class for actual money. My first class where someone literally asked me, in writing, "do you have insurance and a certificate to teach this class?" and I heartily responded with a "Why yes, I certainly do!" (and the email attachment to prove it!)

Every Monday at noon, my company hosts a one-hour yoga class taught by an outside instructor. I love that it's on offer, and it's a great way to break up the workday. No more than about five students ever show up, but I've always loved being one of them.

Today, the usual teacher was out of town. And since I am now on call as the backup teacher, in this moment of crisis they turned to me for help. I'm kind of like Batman, armed with the POWER OF YOGA.

(Random thought: Yogawoman would be a terrible name for a superhero.)

(Random thought #2: Do you think Batman would be less moody if he just gave yoga a chance?)

I only had three students, and boy was I aware the whole time that they were co-workers. I was SUPER nervous, much more than I'd have expected to be. The thing about teaching strangers is that if they don't like your teaching, they just won't come back to your class and you'll never have to see them again. And if you teach friends and do a crappy job, well, they'll probably still love you. Whereas if you teach colleagues, you still have to see them every day.

Fortunately it all went fine. All three of them complimented me once we'd finished, and one even came by my desk later in the afternoon to tell me again how much she'd enjoyed it, at which point I pretty much dissolved into twin pools of relief and gratitude.

I'm actually not even sure how much I earned from teaching today. I think about £24 pre-tax, so not exactly a fortune, but still! It's not about money--it's about experience and practice on doing something that I absolutely love sharing with others.........and seeing wherever it may lead me.

Love,

Joëlle

Side note: I couldn't believe how nervous I was teaching this class. I literally wanted to run away screaming. But as I started teaching it on a weekly basis, things got much better a lot quicker than I'd have expected. Soon, I wasn't nervous at all, and was even looking forward to it every week!

So again, if you can just dive in to a scary situation and give the first couple of times a whirl, you are very likely to surprise yourself.

~~~~~

Tying Up Loose Ends

There were many more yoga blog entries in my year of Happy Moments, even after my training completed. I wrote about taking on yoga challenges on Instagram, and attending a yoga show, and taking an inversions workshop, and reading yoga magazines, and meeting a yoga celebrity, and – on one slightly more esoteric day – healing my qi. Some of those experiences (such as teaching that first, nerve-wracking class!) were obviously more challenging than others. But the true challenge for me was actually just *doing* it in the first place – something I didn't think I could do, and yet I did it anyway.

My yoga teacher training was one of the best decisions I've ever made. And not just because of how much I enjoyed the yoga itself, but because of the challenge. This was not something I was ever "supposed" to do. It wasn't something that everyone in my inner circle understood. It isn't something that (so far) has made me much money – in fact, I've yet to make back anything close to the cost of the course itself. And it definitely wasn't easy. Dealing with injury, putting lots of other activities and personal pleasures on hold, waking up early every day to practice...it was *hard*. And that made it all the more rewarding.

Perhaps my biggest takeaway from the entire experience – and one I think can benefit anyone who wants to try something new and challenging – is this: You *are* able to do it. I was scared and uncertain and had lots of reasons not to do it, and I did it anyway. You can too. Chances are, like me, some part of you already knows that you can. Perhaps that's what's so disappointing about those many challenges we never do end up undertaking: We know that we actually could do them, if it weren't for that pesky fear. If only we just jumped.

So I encourage anyone – the next time a challenge comes up, something you actually want to do – just do it. Don't overthink it. That's how I ended up ultimately kind of falling into the yoga teacher training: I went to an info session, they happened to have an open slot the very next week, and before I knew it, I put up my hand and that slot was mine. I didn't even really have time to overthink it. I just jumped.

Small voice piping up: *"And what if I can't jump? What if nothing changes? What if I just can't?"*

Even smaller, yet frightfully stubborn voice: *"But you CAN. You can do things that seemed impossible 100 days ago or 3 years ago or yesterday. You can do things that feel impossible right now and that might be unthinkable tomorrow and you can do them anyway because YES YOU CAN and because EVERYTHING*

CHANGES. Always, always, always. Just keep swimming."

That, right there, was the belief that kept me going on all of those "What if I just *can't*" days. That 'frightfully stubborn' voice that just wouldn't shut up. And even after finishing my yearlong blog in its original incarnation, that voice is probably the biggest thing that has stayed with me beyond it. It's the reason I keep setting goals and tackling challenges – no, I haven't accomplished every single one of them, but even for those I haven't, I've gotten closer than if I hadn't set them at all. I've gotten – and stayed – a lot happier than if I'd never started looking for Happy Moments. I've made real changes in my life, and they are changes I wanted.

On a subsequent, but related entry – on September 22nd – I wrote the following:

"And I think if there's maybe one thing that this whole blogging experience has taught me thus far, it's this: You really do get out of life what you put into it. Seriously.

It's not earth-shattering news, but it's true. Want to start a blog, even though you always failed before? Guess what: You can. Want to write every day, even though you don't know what the Hell you're talking about? Write anyway and discover along the way. Want to be a yoga teacher even though you can't even do a headstand yet? Do it anyway and learn. Want to visit somewhere, try something, meet someone? Then GO! DO! ACT!"

It was that same frightfully stubborn voice rearing up again, beating the inside of my head like a drum to keep me on my ACTION TOWARDS CHANGE AND HAPPINESS path.

If you've ever had a stubborn voice like that inside your head, listen to it. Don't ever quiet it. It may be the loudest, most encouraging cheerleader you'll ever meet.

And I wish everyone much cliff-jumping in their future.

~~~~~

Prompt 6: Challenging Yourself – Because Nobody Said This Was Easy

This is all about stepping – nay, leaping – off cliffs to pursue the challenges and quests that interest you, fear and uncertainty be damned! What are the ones you wish *you* could pursue? Is there a degree, or course, or physical accomplishment you'd like to achieve? Maybe it's finishing a 10K, maybe it's learning a new language, maybe it's an additional certification to help with your career. What makes you nervous? What have you said no to in the past because, ostensibly, you didn't have enough time/money/talent, when in fact some part of you knows that isn't true? What are you already doing that you could give yourself more credit for?

Things I'd like to do, or have wanted to undertake in the past are _____

_____

_____

Reasons I haven't undertaken those things before include _____

_____

_____

Why do I want to do these things? What's driving the desire in the first place? _____

_____

_____

One thing I already do regularly, even when I don't feel like it, is _____. The reason I do it even when I really don't want to is _____.
Afterwards, I feel _____ because _____

_____.

The first step I would need to take to pursue my most desired challenge is (in other words, what's that step that takes you off the cliff and into the void) _____

_____

_____

Copy the following statement (or another similarly-affirmative one of your choice): "I pledge to jump off this cliff. I know that some part of me believes I can do this, and that there is a net of some kind waiting for me on the way down. I know that achieving this will be scary and require effort, and I know that this fear does not define me." _____

_____

_____

Chapter 7: Forming Happy Habits

Aka the "Look, I can do better!" chapter.

High on the list of things I have struggled with my entire life is the formation of positive habits. Habits do not come easily to me. Habits are similar to challenges, by the way, except they're more routine and ritualistic, and can therefore be tackled a little differently from the "big" types of challenges covered in the previous chapter.

For whatever reason, I have always been a relatively disciplined person: I can show up on time, I can wake up early, I can complete assignments. But what I struggle with is focus. It's almost like I need an external motivator to actually get those things done that I don't *need* to get done, like completing New Year's-style resolutions or creating healthier rituals for myself.

For example, this book! The fact that you're even reading it is nothing short of a miracle to me, given how many months it spent as a vague concept in my mind, without a single word being written. It was only once a friend of mine proposed a creativity accountability group that I started to make regular, painstaking progress— where before I'd had nothing more than an introduction and the oft-repeated desire that, "Oh, I'd really like to write a book someday."

The experience writing this book only supplemented these types of observations about myself, which I'd already noted during my year of Happy Moments. Namely, that I don't tend to struggle with *daily* discipline. Time and time again, I'd have friends ask me about my blog: "But isn't it hard to write *every* day?" and the truth was – for me – it really wasn't. I think I'd actually have struggled more with the idea of writing just once a week, or writing only every time I had a great idea. Simply writing every day meant I just had to do it, and that wasn't especially difficult. Even on those days when I didn't have the foggiest clue of what to write about, I knew I was still going to get it done, even if that meant setting my alarm for a little earlier than normal, or putting off going to bed for another 20 minutes.

And writing wasn't the only good habit I formed. I wrote down new ideas every day. I meditated. I read more books. I traveled to places I'd wanted to see but hadn't made the effort to. I went on more local adventures and got to know London, the city I lived in. The more I wrote about all of these things, the more I wanted successes to show for my efforts. The more I wanted to live, rather than just watch time pass me by.

I realize not everyone is like this. We all form habits in different ways, and some (unbelievably lucky) people probably don't even need external motivators at all. But what helps is to recognize ourselves for these personal strengths and weaknesses, and exploit them for all they're worth. For me, that means I need to work on something every freaking day if I want to get it done, because even missing one day could cause me to lose my focus completely.

One thing I actually found super-helpful was to do a retrospective at the end of every month: since I'd have 30 (or so, depending on the month) Happy Moments to look back on, that helped put that month into perspective as to what I'd actually achieved. That made that month matter, and seeing how disciplined I'd been at various pursuits during that month increased my focus and improved my habits even further.

A few of those illustrations of how I formed my better habits:

~~~~~

January 21st: 21 Days of Blogging

There is a common, oft-repeated belief that it takes 21 days to form a new habit. Listerine has a challenge built around it. Popsugar claims it can banish your belly fat. Even Jay-Z and Beyoncé used it to attempt veganism.

In other words, want to quit smoking/give up sugar/exercise more/wake up earlier? Simply commit to doing it for 21 days in a row, and voilà, *a new habit is formed. Trick your brain into thinking it's temporary, in other words, and after three weeks, your brain will* want *to do the new thing all on its own.*

While the 21-day-belief system has pretty much been proven to be a myth (it's more like an average of 66 days), I still think it's worth a check-in now that I've been blogging for 21 days straight. I'd never even written one *blog post before January 1st. In fact, I didn't start this one with the intention of writing more than 'maybe every once in a while,' whatever that meant.*

But I've always wanted *to start one, or at least write more than before, which is...well, not much. I've always wanted more creative outlets; I've just been fearful to try them. Pursuing a traditional, corporate, and, frankly, boring path always seemed like the safer option. It's why I did the things I was 'supposed to', like get an MBA, work in banking, and so on.*

But I guess the thing is...says who? Who am I 'supposed' to do these things for, really? Not my parents. Not my friends. Not "society." So maybe it's time to listen a little more closely to what genuinely excites me, and right now, my little blog is doing that. For 21 days, I've thought to myself, what shall I write about today? *I've noticed little things in my day, like the sun breaking through the clouds, or Vegemite! I've listened to random thoughts in my head, like,* Could 'Ode to a stepstool' be a compelling blog post? *(Doubtful.)* I like *this feeling of excitement. It's new and strange and fun. It makes me want more of it.*

I have no idea how many more days in a row I'll blog. I hope a lot. I hope I make it to 66 days, or maybe beyond, though I'm not quite ready to officially commit to that. But I have 21 Happy Moments to show for this experiment so far, and if that's not a habit, at least it'll be a good memory.

Love,

Joëlle

Side note: I love re-reading that particular entry, because – unbeknownst to me at the time – those 21 days would become the first baby steps of my entire year of Happy Moments. It was barely the first 5%! And yet I already felt so good about it! I think that's a great reminder to myself and to anyone else out there: If something gives you that feeling of excitement and happiness, keep doing it. Even if it doesn't "make sense." Just keep going and see what it becomes, and get a little bit closer to knowing yourself along the way. I can't recommend it enough.

~~~~~

January 31st: Fare Thee Well, January

Somewhat unbelievably, we are now at the end of the year's first month. So how has 2016 gone so far? Let's see:

- I've started my first blog (hurray!) and written 31 days in a row

- I've suffered and started my recovery from my first actual injury in years

- I've meditated 31 days in a row

- I started 30 days of yoga camp, had to drop out, and tentatively started again. I'm now 9 gentle days in on take #2.

- I've read 2 new books, and listened to 2 new audiobooks

- I've traveled to Venice and Milan for the first time

- I've opened a UK savings account

- I am hours away from successfully completing Dry January

Favorite moment of the month: Wandering around the island of Burano, marveling at the beauty of a place I hadn't known existed 48 hours earlier.

Quote of the month: "Stop going to the hardware store for milk."

All in all, I'd say that's a pretty good start. 2016, I like you. You can stay.

Love,
Joëlle

Side note: I wrote an entry like this one at the end of every month, and I have to say, they really helped me stay on track! Previously, I always had a tendency to write New Year's resolutions at the beginning of a year, but then I'd typically either never look at them again, or otherwise I'd come across them sometime in late November and think, "Well, crap. I forgot I was going to do all of that, and now it's too late, so I may as well not even try."

Looking back on the Happy Moments from the prior month helped me stay focused on my good habits, and also reminded me of how much I had to be happy about.

~~~~~

May 15th: My Monkey Mind

Loyal fans of my blog (a just-barely-plural community, but growing nevertheless!) may remember that on January 1st this year, I set a goal to meditate every single day in 2016. 136 days into the year, I am simultaneously very proud that I've kept true to that goal thus far, and FREAKING FRUSTRATED THAT

THIS IS TOO HARD AND WHY CAN'T I SHUT OFF MY BRAIN AND THIS DOESN'T FEEL ANY EASIER THAN IT DID FIVE MONTHS AGO AND OH MY AAHUHGUSHFDHCNIOHWTOHFID!!!

So...you can see it's working.

Meditation is often said to help quiet the "monkey mind," a reference to how the mind can jump around from one topic to another, never staying still, constantly screeching.

Let me tell you, 136 days in, my monkey is still climbing as many trees, swinging from as many branches, and flinging as much poop as he ever did. (My monkey is definitely male, by the way.)

This morning, I crossed 24 hours in total meditation time since the beginning of the year on the Calm app. (I've actually done more than that since I do occasionally use other apps, but still, 24 hours is a nice round number.)

That's one whole day, broken down into more-or-less 10-minute segments across almost five months. That's a whole day of at least trying to be calm. Of trying to visualize calm spaces, beaches, quiet streams, rainbows, shooting beams of golden light, and the like.

A whole day of repeating mantras to myself: "I am just one step away from something incredible. I am so much more than my thoughts. I can create a positive charge. May I be happy. I let go of that which doesn't serve me. Cultivate the fire within you. External change flows from the inside. Compassion and acceptance. The scariest thing in life is the thing you never start." (You get the idea.)

Some days it reallyreallyreally feels like I've made zero progress.

And then I remember, I didn't use to be able to sit still for 10 minutes at a time. Now I can. I didn't use to remember positive thoughts and phrases. And now (on my better days) I do. So...maybe this is all slowly, slowly, ever-so-slowly moving me towards a happier, calmer life.

And maybe eventually, that monkey will get off my back.

Love,

Joëlle

Side note: When trying to form better habits, there is an unfortunate – and frustrating – reality that sometimes that's just *hard*. And you don't always feel like you're making progress. I felt like that with meditating, and writing, and so many other things that year. It's hard to keep plugging along sometimes, particularly if there's something you're trying to do every day.

So I think it's helpful to regularly remind yourself of why you're trying to form that better habit in the first place. For me, I wanted to live a happier life, and I wanted to see if habits like daily meditation could get me closer. So even on those days when it was super difficult, I could still find 10 minutes a day to devote to that broader aim, even if that particular meditation session felt agonizing and pointless.

So if you too have a broader aim – like wanting to be happier, or calmer, or stronger – don't give up just because you had one difficult session. Don't let it all go just because today's effort felt like a waste of time. Keep asking yourself why you wanted to do this in the first place. See if maybe an adjustment is required in your approach to this new habit. Ask yourself what you've learned so far.

The answer might surprise you.

~~~~~

July 2nd: Checking in on Resolutions

Now that we're officially into the second half of the year, the time seems right to check in on the New Year's resolutions I set back in January. I haven't really looked at these since then, mind you, but hey, there's still another almost-six months to go, so let's see how we're doing!

Because I'm kind of a nerd, I had split them into 4 buckets: Physical, Mental, Emotional, and Spiritual. So let's take those one at a time.

(**Side note:** Don't worry, I'm only including a few key resolutions in this book out of a looooooong list!)

Physical

- _Run 600km - This is a tough one to swallow. Back in 2015, I ran 1,352km. Whereas this year, I'm going to struggle to hit even half that, mostly due to my hamstring injury. Currently sitting pretty at 251._
- _Get certified in yoga - I didn't even remember I had actually put this in here! And look at me now: by tomorrow night I'll be 80% of the way there! Unbelievable! Hard work pays off._
- _Learn to do a headstand - Hey! Ticked this box too!_
- _Complete Dry January – Tick!_
- _Drink at least 1.5L of water per day – Doing well at this too._

Mental

- _Quit my job – This remains a huge box to tick._
- _Get my MBA loan down to less than $10K - It was an aggressive number, but still an outsider's chance before the end of the year._

- Spend mindfully - I'm all over this. Write my expenditures down in my daily planner and everything, like a total nerd.

- Start a blog - Hahahahahaha! If I had only known then what I know now! ;-)

Emotional

- Only check Instagram, Facebook, and other social media once a day - I started out great on this, but have stumbled in the past two months or so. Still, it's fixable!

- Meet my future husband - I mean, I'm sure he's on his way. (**Side note:** I started dating Steffen two months after writing this entry, so this may actually prove true!)

- Keep one night a week sacred to spend on taking care of myself - This is probably THE resolution I've completely neglected this year, and I still think it's a good one. One to work on.

Spiritual

- Start meditating - Done!

- Carry around my 2016 planner. Fill it with beautiful memories. - I actually do write down memories and quotes in the little planner next to my bed, and I love it! Such great retrospectives for the future!

- Take one trip every month - Done! Trips so far have included Milan/Venice, Switzerland, Malta, India, and

more! Next month I'll be heading to New York and Washington, DC.

- Take time to be grateful. Remember the BEST thing that happened to me each and every day. – This is always the last thing I do at night as I'm falling asleep.

Wow! So how am I doing so far in 2016? Well...generally pretty well, it would seem! Sure, there's lots to work on, and probably even some goals to readjust, or even a few new ones to add. I'm not exactly the same person I was on January 1st.

I am officially adding one here, for the record: I want to write a blog post for every day of 2016. This is a huge goal, but now that I'm halfway there, it isn't outside the realm of possibility. It feels achievable. It feels big. It feels proud. It feels like me. So I'm going on record to say: Yup. I'm doing it.

(**Side note:** I did do it, and it feels great!)

Not all resolutions are kept. A 2013 Forbes study said only 8% of New Year's Resolutions were actually achieved.[4] So, probably a good idea for those of us who want to form better habits to check in now and then and see how we're doing. Tonight was a great exercise for that reason.

In any case, 2016 is shaping out to be one hell of a year. Right?

Love,

Joëlle

Side note: I think it's valuable for anyone who wants to form better habits, or set and achieve new goals, to find the best way of checking in that works for them. Maybe it's writing your goals down, maybe it's having an accountability buddy you can catch up with on a regular basis, maybe it's using some sort of carrot-and-stick reward/punishment system for yourself. Be flexible with your goals, too: some may no longer be as meaningful as they once were; some may be worth continuing to push for; some may take a little longer than previously expected; and some may prove to actually be easier than you thought, leading you to wonder why you'd never attempted them before!

Another point is that it's best not to spend too much time wondering, "where has the time gone?" when you're checking in, and instead ask yourself "what am I going to do with the time left?" The past is the past, and it can inform us and make us smile, yes, but looking back too much can also inspire guilt or even fear if the past didn't look exactly how we may have wanted it to.

We can always dwell on what we "should" have done with the time gone by, but where does that really get us? Much better to take an honest, motivated, and positive approach towards the time we have left. Onwards and upwards!

~~~~~

December 31st: Once Upon a December

It's. Here.

The ultimate day of the year. I really, honestly, cannot believe it.

There's so much to process. We haven't even poured the champagne yet for tonight's celebration, and I'm already lost in reflection about the 2016 year that's flickering to an end.

But you know what? I feel like December often gets short shrift when we get to the end of the year. There's a tendency to look at the year as a whole, and since I did after all reflect back at the end of all 11 previous months this year, I think December deserves its due. So today I'm going to write a 'normal' end-of-month post.

Then tomorrow, January 1st, I'm going to write a more introspective look back at my one-year blogging experiment, and maybe touch on a few hopes and dreams for 2017.

And then two days from now, on January 2nd, after 367 straight days ... I'm not going to blog. I feel strange, kind of sad, unbelievably relieved, and even a little tingly just thinking about it.

But for now, enough about that! As promised, I'll turn my thoughts back to December to honor the following Happy Moments:

- 366 straight days of blogging (oh my gosh ... I actually did it)

- 270/366 days of meditation (fell off the wagon halfway through, then jumped back on)

- I traveled to Hamburg once ... twice ... three times!

- For my very last trip of the year, I explored a little more of northern Germany, visiting the island of Sylt

- I fêted several important people in my life, including my Dad, my Mom, and my boyfriend

- I got a brand new travel buddy in the form of a shiny red passport

- There were Christmas celebrations galore, including the office holiday party, Christmas Jumper Day, my grandfather's 98th birthday party on December 24th, and Christmas itself (duh)

- And finally, as we head into the New Year, I found inspiration twice over: first, through my inspired Dear Diary; and second, through my friend Yin's beautiful candle brand launch.

Favorite moment of the month: As always, quite a few to choose from this month. But simply because of where I am in life, and wanting to really absorb some inspiration for the end of the year, I'm going to give it to the ANDAS candle launch. I was just so impressed, and it was great to see "real" people doing "real" things like that.

Quote of the month: "It won't be forever. You'll be in the dark as long as it takes and then you'll come out."
~ Finding Audrey[5]

Goal for next month/year: Well, again, remember that 2017 planner/diary for an inspired year? I want to start making it proud.

And that's it for 2016. An amazing year, topped off by 31 final Happy Moments. Thanks for those, December.

And now, time to pop the champagne!
Love,
Joëlle

Side note: It's great seeing the habits that stood out across the entire year. Again, this hammers home the importance of staying focused on happier habits.

~~~~~

Tying Up Loose Ends

Writing this chapter cemented the importance of FOCUS for me in forming good habits. We may not achieve each and every goal that we originally set for ourselves: after all, sometimes things take a little longer, and sometimes we realize a goal is no longer as important as it used to be, and we choose to focus somewhere else instead. But that focus itself IS important. In other words, it's necessary to go in some sort of direction, even if you don't know exactly when and where the journey will end.

I found two elements to be particularly useful as I worked on achieving better focus – and forming better habits – during my year of Happy Moments: Daily effort, and forgiveness.

The daily effort was necessary for me in order to *stay* focused – chipping away towards a goal each and every day made it seem more approachable, and just a little bit closer every time I took one more baby step.

The forgiveness element was just as important: Expending any energy or time making myself feel bad was not helpful. And I am GOOD at guilt! I'm a PRO at it: "Joëlle, why didn't you do this in your twenties?" "Why didn't you get it done when you said you would?" "You're basically the oldest person ever to think about doing this, so why are you even here?" (As if being in your mid-thirties were some sort of deathbed.) Again, just like in Chapter 1: Silence those cruel voices! Use forgiveness to let thoughts like that go and just move on with what it is you want to do. Because the thing is, there's never any turning back the clock. Your next birthday is still coming, and it'll be that much closer tomorrow. So do you want to spend the next 24 hours wishing you were younger and more "accomplished" (whatever that means), or do you want to forgive any perceived slights by your past self and work on making your future self that much more capable and happy?

My sister told me about an exercise once, which I try to use anytime those nasty voices come back, telling me I "should" have done something differently. It's very simple: Inside your own head, say a few quick words of forgiveness to yourself: "I love you. I'm sorry. Please forgive me." It literally takes two seconds, and as long as you keep doing it, you'll become more and more accepting of yourself, every time.

Forgiveness, daily baby steps, and focus remain at the heart of all the good habits and achievements I continue to strive for, and I have found them to be loyal partners in getting just a little bit closer to who I would like to be.

Perhaps they can help you too.

~~~~~

Prompt 7: Forming Happy Habits

These exercises are all about finding what works for YOU to form better habits and find better focus. When have you been successful at working on goals in the past? What were the elements that helped you make progress? What gets in the way of you sticking to good habits – Time? Other things getting in the way? Changing goals? What could you do differently to challenge these potential pitfalls?

Examples of goals I have worked towards successfully in the past are (and don't you dare say you haven't successfully achieved any goals, because that's just not true. Have you learned a new skill or language? Mastered a sport? Obtained a degree? Planned an event? Keep writing!) _____

_____

_____

Why was I successful in them? What were the elements that I ultimately found helpful? _____

_____

_____

What elements have stood in the way of my being successful on other goals? _____

_____

_____

What success-linked elements could I apply to future goals, in order to form happy habits? _____

_____

_____

What are the habits I would LIKE to have? _____

_____

_____

Can I forgive myself, here and now, for potentially not having always had absolutely perfect habits in the past? (Hint: The answer is "YES.") _____

_____

_____

Chapter 8: Find the Happy in Random

Aka, the "Oh, *yeah!* That happened!" chapter.

We all have little random things that happen to us every day. We overhear a stranger on the bus say something silly on the phone. We're offered free samples of the newest soft drink on the market by brightly dressed teenagers as we walk down the street. We end up using a different coffee mug in the office because the one we usually use has disappeared. We decide to make a slightly different dinner one night because the supermarket runs out of that one ingredient we'd normally use.

None of these occurrences is particularly "important," certainly not in the grand scheme of life, and often times we forget about these just a few minutes after they've happened.

But in my quest to find something happy and distinctive about every single day for a year, I started being more curious and paying a lot of attention to moments like these. I found totally random moments to actually be a huge source of happiness! Something you could casually smile about, and that – even months later – could still cause an "Oh, *yeah!* That happened!"

moment. They were little moments I could call back on, particularly in times of frustration, that would sometimes allow me to simply roll my eyes at whatever was irritating me right then and there, and just move on.

A few examples:

~~~~~

January 28th: Annona Reticulata?

I bought a new fruit today. Custard apples were on sale, my local market proclaimed! From £2.49 down to 99p - practically a steal!

Now I've never actually heard of a custard apple before, but based on the helpful panel tacked to the box they were in, I'd have had to be a fool to not buy one! Why, according to the sign, these babies:

a) help in neutralizing free radicals

b) are good for hair, eyes, and healthy skin

c) relax muscles

d) can be applied on ulcers, abscesses and boils

e) treat dysentery

f) serve as an expectorant

g) have insecticidal seeds

...and so much more!

They're essentially like a dose of healthy magic, for less than a pound. (I mean, they're not healthy for the insects, obviously. But they'll basically cure everything else.)

Upon getting home from the market I eagerly looked up custard apples on Wikipedia and found out it's the common name for annona reticulata, generally found growing in Central America and Southeast Asia.

Only...hang on, the fruit I bought doesn't look like the picture on Wikipedia. ...Nor like the photos in Google images. Nor....come to think of it...like the picture on the magic-proclaiming sign itself. And...continuing with my cracking investigation here, when I cut it open, there are no insecticidal seeds. *More like one giant, probably-not-fatal-to-insects pit.*

... Yeah, that's a mango. I bought a mango. For £2.49.

I just hope I don't catch dysentery now.

Love,

Joëlle

Side note: This was one of those totally ridiculous moments where I obviously "screwed up" – I mean, I DO know what a mango looks like! – and yet I think it ended up being a much better outcome than if I hadn't. In other words, if I HAD actually bought a real custard apple, I don't think I'm likely to have enjoyed it nearly as much as I did buying a fake one.

So whenever we make little "mistakes" like this, I think it's always worth asking ourselves if we can find some humor in the situation. Something silly to take away from it that makes us smile. I still smile sometimes if I see a mango because I'm remembering this very incident. Chances are, there are similar incidents in your life that could also be used to brighten up future days.

~~~~~

February 20th: Follow the White Rabbit

There are approximately 888 English Heritage blue plaques scattered across London, marking where famous people have lived and worked, and intended to celebrate their achievements. I've noticed them all over the place, generally referencing people I've never heard of. And yesterday morning, on my walk to work, one in particular caught my eye:

"WING COMMANDER F.F.E. YEO-THOMAS GC 1902-1964

Secret Agent codename 'The White Rabbit' lived here"

'What's this?' I asked myself. 'Could it be...mystery? Intrigue? Perhaps even a quest?!?'

Yes, while I've never heard of F.F.E. Yeo-Thomas, there are few things I love more than delving into a good quest. So today, I'm delving! I found some fairly-detailed tidbits on his Wikipedia page:[6]

- *F.F.E. stood for Forest Frederick Edward, though he went by "Tommy" (which I found incomprehensibly hilarious until I realized it's undoubtedly in reference to his surname).*

- *He moved to France with his family early in life, allowing him to pass as a French national while spying in Occupied France during World War II.*

- *He personally convinced Winston Churchill to provide resources to the French resistance.*

- *In March 1944, he was betrayed, brutally tortured by the Gestapo, sent to Buchenwald concentration camp, then Stalag prisoner-of-war camp, before repeatedly escaping and finally reaching allied lines in April 1945. He never named names or gave up any secrets.*

- *He survived the war and was a key witness at the Nuremberg War Trials in the identification of Buchenwald officials.*

- *After the war, he went to work - of all places - at a Paris fashion house.*

- *The 'GC' on the blue plaque means he was awarded the George Cross, the second-highest* honor in the United Kingdom, and the highest award for civilians.

What was missing from Wikipedia was why he was codenamed 'The White Rabbit.' And so I delved on.

The Telegraph provided a fascinating story: Yeo-Thomas was the inspiration for James Bond![7] Ian Fleming - who also worked for British intelligence in the war - even wrote a memo about old Tommy, who apparently was also a bit of a ladies' man.

(...I suppose "Bond. James Bond." does roll off the tongue a bit more easily than "Yeo-Thomas. Forest Frederick Edward Yeo-Thomas." But I digress.)

A Daily Mail article[8] describes the 2010 unveiling of his plaque at the Bloomsbury home he shared with his common-law wife starting in 1941. He was actually still married to his legal wife—scandalous!

I never did find a source that stated conclusively why the Germans codenamed him The White Rabbit. It's the title of both a miniseries and a book based on his exploits. I suppose - much like the white rabbit from Lewis Carroll's Wonderland - he'd sometimes simply, mysteriously disappear into the underground.

I'm glad to see him recognized. You never know what a blue plaque might teach you about history, and heroes.

Love,
Joëlle

Side note: Admittedly this one involved further research, so it's perhaps not *completely* random, but it still started out by simply keeping my eyes open and staying curious on my walk to work.

One could argue that knowing a lot more about someone like Yeo-Thomas isn't exactly useful information five decades after his death, but to that I'd answer, "Oh, and what did YOU notice during YOUR commute to work today?" So many of us have activities that we repeat over and over and over to the point of tedium, and I'd argue it's much better to liven those activities up where we can with a little intrigue and a smile or two. Even if I hadn't done any further research on Yeo-Thomas, in fact, I'd still have learned that someone with a Secret Agent codename had lived in my neighborhood, and that's already rather fun.

So again, stay curious even when repeating something for what feels like the millionth time, and you really might learn something!

~~~~~

March 14th: Colors and Pumpkins and Yoko Ono

The bus stop in front of my building has a new advertisement today.

I was intrigued as I approached it, coming home from a (if I do say so myself) well-deserved round of drinks with a colleague.

At first I thought it was Psy, the South Korean "Gangnam Style" rapper, with giant oranges floating around his head.

Then as I drew closer, I thought it might be Yoko Ono, also with giant oranges floating around her head.

When I was finally standing squarely in front of it, I determined it was neither. It's a non-famous woman (I think) lying down in a pumpkin patch, photographed on an iPhone 6S by that most elusive of photographers, Timothy M, in an advertisement for Apple.

So, first of all, I want to apologize to the model, whoever she is, for thinking she was:

a) A slightly-paunchy male rapper; and

b) An 83-year-old woman.

Up close, it is clear she is neither.

Second, I want to have a little moment of gratitude for the brightness of the colors that met me outside my front door. Coming home from a rather gray day, this was just the little breath of fresh air I needed.

Love,

Joëlle

Side note: I remember the exact moment I first noticed this advertisement. I'd had a pretty bad day at work, and I was grumbling to myself that I didn't want to write a blog entry when I got home, and didn't have any ideas to write about. And I was literally about ten steps from my front door when I came across the ad, which provided me not only with something to write about, but also a much-needed smile and reminder that things really weren't that bad.

You never know what might cheer you up or provide a Happy Moment. An advertisement, a telemarketer, a piece of fruit, a trip to the bathroom... It really is all about staying curious and open-minded as you notice the little things around you.

~~~~~

July 25th: I Must Upgrade my Toilet

Ok, I have got to get me one of these.

This, my friends, is the Toto Washlet SG. It is glorious.

I was at dinner with my friend Claudia at Sosharu, a chic Japanese restaurant in Farringdon. The food was fabulous: steamed octopus, rice hot pots,

Asian pears marinated in miso sauce... delicious. Towards the end of the meal, Claudia excused herself to go to the bathroom.

She was gone quite a while. And when she finally came back, her eyes were sparkling.

"You must go to the toilet. It's amazing." she told me in a whisper, as if code-speaking some sort of drug deal.

"Whyyyyy?" I asked hesitantly, worried about what I'd find there.

"Just go," she said again. I swear she winked.

With some trepidation, I made my way downstairs and found the loo. What I found there was, in fact, amazing. Oh, Toto Washlet SG, where have you been all my life?

It's probably obvious at this point that I'm talking about a Japanese toilet. And I have had the pleasure of experiencing those before (gosh, this is getting personal).

But...not quite like this. Think seat warmers. Think sensor-activated lid. Think warm water jets with adjustable pressure. Think dryer. Think remote control. Think antibacterial electrolyzed personal cleansing system!

I stayed in there rather a long time myself. Pressing each and every button at least once. Mentally

143

wondering the entire time whether there'd be any chance of talking my landlord into buying me a new toilet that retails for £4,700. I mean, I have been a good tenant.

"You were right," I said to Claudia when I finally came back upstairs.

"It's amazing."

Love,

Joëlle

Side note: If you can't get a kick out of something like a Japanese toilet, believe me: you're taking life too seriously. Maximize those random encounters where you can, and definitely stay curious!

~~~~~

October 20th: My Very First Fan

I've just replied to - in a matter of speaking - my first fan mail.

Every so often, I get a couple of likes on one of my blog posts. Anything above 3 is always SUPER exciting, because it means that in addition to my mom, my sister, and my best friend, someone else is reading my blog!!!

Every once in a while, one of those three people will even post a comment, and that's even MORE exciting because: feedback!

But imagine my surprise when I was notified this week that I had a comment on one of my posts ("Tubeless where possible") and for the first time ever, I didn't know who it was from.

"Nice writing... love reading your posts." someone named Anamika wrote.

I don't think I've ever met anyone by that name, but I simply can't tell you how thrilling this was. I really haven't marketed my blog at all, beyond a couple of Twitter and Facebook posts. I'd love for it to grow (and for myself to grow as a writer, come to that), and it's absolutely on me that I haven't put much effort into it. Any feedback or praise or encouragement is always so appreciated, because I still struggle all the time with the quintessential questions of, "why am I doing this?" and "is this worth it in any way?"

I'm not sure how Anamika found my blog in the first place - perhaps just one of those random Internet stumbles we all have once in a while, but this, truly was the textbook definition of a Happy Moment for me.

So Anamika, if you are reading this, you really did make my day. Thank you.

Love,

Joëlle

Side note: In this case, I was basically able to find happiness in someone *else's* random stumble. You just never know what might bring people together – even virtually, and even for the briefest of moments sometimes.

This particular experience, also, highlights to me the importance of expressing gratitude and compliments. Anamika didn't have to leave me a comment, but by taking 30 seconds to do so, she honestly made my day. And I hope that by expressing some gratitude to her in a new blog post, I helped make *her* day a little happier. Because happiness is definitely something that can be passed on and shared, even to people you've never actually met.

So don't skimp! Compliment someone today. Say a sincere thank you to that person who helped you out, or made you smile. Chances are, you'll improve both their day and yours, no matter how random the encounter.

~~~~~

Tying Up Loose Ends

I think in some ways this was the "easiest" chapter concept for me to follow, because it didn't actually require me doing anything. I'd just kind of go about my normal days, and see what random circumstances would come my way. All I'd have to do was stay curious, notice them, and make a little mental note that, "Hey, that was kind of fun." A little extra gratitude where appropriate helped prolong that happy feeling.

How often do we tend to dwell on negative random occurrences, but completely dismiss the positive ones as stupid and coincidental?

Think about it: Don't we tend to remember things like that time we didn't quite like that one coworker's tone (which, come to think of it, may have been a misunderstanding)? Or that time we just missed the bus and there wasn't another one for a whole gosh-darn eight minutes? Or that time we went to our favorite restaurant and they were out of the appetizer we'd been looking forward to ordering, and it basically ruined the entire meal? All of these things really are *random,* and yet our minds can sometimes make such a big deal out of them! If we could spend even just half as much brainpower and energy capturing and noticing random *good* moments, wouldn't that help counterbalance an awful lot of negativity? I think so.

So again, keep your eyes open. Be interested in the little things around you. Look people in the eye. If you think something is beautiful, or funny, or interesting, say so – even if it's just inside your own head. If someone provides you with a little random moment of happiness, thank them if it's appropriate. See what starts to come your way, and notice if perhaps you're smiling just a little bit more often – surprise yourself!

And stay random, my friends.

~~~~~

Prompt 8: Find the Happy in Random

This chapter is all about bringing the random, "accidental" Happy Moments to the forefront, noticing them, observing them, and storing them in our memory banks for later. What random examples in your everyday life could serve as sources of happiness? What could you notice as you go about your daily activities to file away as a silly memory? How could you do that a little more often to make these moments stand out and turn a so-called "normal" day into something that's maybe just a little more exciting?

Something random that happened to me in the past 3 days and made me smile is _____

_____

_____

The most random thing that happened to me today (or yesterday, if it's early in the morning) is _____

_____

_____

How could I turn that particular random moment into a happy memory? _____

_____

_____

How would I LIKE to react to random, silly moments in the future? _____

_____

_____

What could I do differently the next time something random happens to me? _____

_____

_____

Chapter 9: What About When I Feel Sad?

Aka, the "This too shall pass" chapter.

It's all well and good to have gotten through the past eight chapters and thought about noticing random little fun moments, things that make YOU happy, time with friends and family, exciting adventures and challenges and happy habits, and the like. But what about those days where – for whatever reason – you just feel sad? Let's call these (creative naming alert) Sad Days.

You may know the types of Sad Days (or moments) that I'm talking about. The ones where it's not even necessarily that something sad or especially difficult has happened... It's just that for some reason, on this particular day, you can't do this. You're feeling kind of blue. You're over it. Something inside of you just kind of hurts and is taking precedence over everything else around you. You don't want to be wherever you are, doing whatever you're doing. I know I've had a lot of Sad Days like this, and I'd imagine that most of us have them once in a while; because it's pretty much part of what makes us human. In fact, I'd even argue that having the occasional

Sad Day helps make all the happy days a lot more meaningful.

I'd be lying if I said the concept of Those Happy Moments was some sort of cure-all during 2016. I still had sad moments, typically linked to work. Most of those times, I was still able to focus on at least one little positive something from that day – and now when I look back, those are the moments I remember from those days. But there were still a few times where even that felt like too much, and I needed a little something more – and what are you supposed to do with days like that?

Well, from my experience, the first thing to do is to acknowledge how you're feeling. If you feel sad, then allow yourself to be with that sadness, at least for a little while. It's ok to be sad sometimes. Just like it's ok to be angry sometimes, or tired, or disappointed, or frustrated, or whatever it is that you need to feel like at that time. Don't let it take over, necessarily, but do acknowledge it, and ask yourself what might be able to help.

For me, the great news is that I had a LOT (and I mean a LOT) fewer Sad Days in my year of Happy Moments than I'd had in probably any previous year of my life. And the ones I did have, as I said, were mostly linked to work, since I was such a mismatch for my job. But still, simply by focusing a great deal more on happiness that year, I had much less time and space left for sadness.

And for those days when sadness still crept in? I did my best to observe it, and do what I could to address it. And those solutions didn't always have to be terribly sophisticated (cupcakes, anyone?)

Here's how those Sad Days played out for me:

~~~~~

February 1st: Pass me a Spoon

Whenever I've had a particularly long day, perhaps a Manic Monday full of frustrations (like today), whenever I get home and long for a soothing hug from my coat rack, whenever taking a deep cleansing breath just won't quite cut it because I'm too wrapped up in wanting to rock gently back and forth in front of a Harry Potter movie...there is fortunately one go-to that never fails me:

Cupcakes.

Specifically, smushed cupcakes, eaten straight out of the box with a spoon. No plate is necessary. Plates are for dainty people with dainty china accessories who daintily remove their cupcake wrappings before, daintily, nibbling away. Tonight, I was not dainty.

Making an emergency stop at Hummingbird Bakery on my way home (a stone's throw from my house, by the way, which is simultaneously a blessing and a curse), I pondered my two usual top choices: Salted Caramel and Oreo Cookies 'n Cream. Tonight, there was only one left of each. I took that as a sign.

"I'll take them both," I announced decisively, throwing caution, cash, and calories to the wind.

I then went home, put on some Agnes Obel, grabbed a spoon, and dived right in.

Because sometimes, cupcakes just get me.

Love,

Joëlle

Side note: You'll notice that I didn't describe this particular day as especially sad, merely as a day full of frustration. But I do remember that this was a *bad* day – probably one of the worst days I had all year – one of those days where I couldn't take my job anymore, and couldn't see a way out, and even had to go to the bathroom to cry at one point – yes, people really do that.

It was actually deliberate for me to describe the day that way: yes, acknowledging that it certainly wasn't a HAPPY day overall, but refusing to go on for paragraphs of text – or any more thought processes than necessary – about it. Sometimes simply by describing things as slightly better than we feel they are, we take away a little of that sadness' power.

I'd encourage anyone to try it: Give yourself a time limit, or a word count, for how long you're allowed to talk or write about how upset you are. Do the same thing with your thoughts. And have a little happy reward waiting for you at the end of that.

Like, for instance, cupcakes.

~~~~~

March 29th: "Good" Days and "Bad"

This morning, I had what might under certain circumstances be described as an UNhappy moment when I walked back into the office after a fantastic four-day weekend in Malta. Coming back from vacation is never fun, as we all know...the dreaded pile of emails waiting for you, the rain outside when just yesterday you were sunning yourself on a peaceful beach, the desire to smother yourself in pastries when facing a conference call that ughhhhhhhh.

But hey, I always knew it was going to be hard.

So I tried to plan ahead. By coming up with a couple of moments of gratitude I'd be able to hang on to. Little moments of solace on a tough day.

Moment 1: I took a quick coffee break with a friend and co-worker so we could catch up about our respective long weekends and do a bit of brainstorming together.

Moment 2: I took a yoga class at lunchtime. Which felt absolutely terrific. Namaste.

Moment 3: Fine. I ate an entire packet of Maltesers. A large one.

Moment 4: I scheduled a coaching session, which simultaneously gives me a lot of homework coming up and something to really look forward to in terms of life progress.

And, you know, maybe some days that's all we can do. Find the gratitude in the little things. In the things that go wrong. In the "bad" things. Because if we can find gratitude even on days like that, maybe we can start attracting more "good" things our way.

And in the meantime, Maltesers are on sale at Sainsbury's.

Love,

Joëlle

Side note: That little trick of planning small moments of happiness and gratitude for days I KNOW are going to be difficult has served me well since this particular day. I recommend it as a tactic to try!

At the very least, it should help break up the day: see if you can give yourself some sort of mini "reward" for every timespan that you make it through – be it an endless-seeming hour, an annoying phone call, or even just five particularly-difficult minutes. What rewards could you give yourself to look forward to?

~~~~~

June 2nd: Restless Brilliance

I had a really tough day at work today. One of those where you just don't even know what it's all for anymore, and you wish you could chew your way right through your desk and all the way to freedom.

When it was finally time to leave at the end of the day, I tried my usual tactics: I put on a positivity podcast for the walk home, but I kept drowning it out with my own thoughts. I tried some deep breaths. I tried mindfully bringing myself back to the present moment, feeling the cobblestones beneath my feet, noticing the colors and shapes and people around me. Nothing worked.

I was, in a word, feeling restless.

My restlessness took me up a slightly different path home from the one I normally take, just one block off the main road. I've never been on that block before. It took me straight past a sign for the offices of Shine Communications:[9]

"Shine." it advised me. "Stay restless. Be brilliant."

In a perfect world, whenever we're feeling agitated, we'd be able to calm ourselves down. To release anxiety and worries as soon as we've noticed them, to come back to the now, to find perspective and gratitude and poise.

And I am working on that, really. Truly, madly, deeply. I'm doing so much better.

On these days, though, when calm just isn't the word of the day, I love this idea: "Shine. Stay restless. Be brilliant."

I interpret this as an eloquently-phrased version of "Be Yourself." If something isn't working, or if something isn't YOU, change it. Don't favor complacency over restlessness. Look for signs (literally, in this case!), make tweaks, restlessly wrestle yourself towards situations where you CAN shine if that's what feels right in those Restless Moments.

The Happy Moments are still out there, everyday, everywhere.

You just sometimes have to take a restless detour to find them.

Love,

Joëlle

Side note: I still love this sign, and this concept. It's kind of a literal reminder that yes, signs are all around us, and we really can follow them when we're not

157

sure what to do next. And whatever label you want to put on it, whether it's "shining" or something else, do always be yourself. Don't let a Sad Day get in the way of that.

Even if it's just a gentle reminder that "I'm not completely myself today – but I will be again tomorrow. This too shall pass." Because it will. It has to. It always does.

~~~~~

November 10th: Finding A New Normal

It's been a little over 24 hours since I - along with zillions of other people - was shocked to within an inch of my life with the results of the U.S. Presidential election. It still hurts. I was tearing up yesterday thinking about it, and the cold feeling in the pit of my stomach hasn't completely disappeared yet.

And yet, there was a feeling of normalcy again in parts of last night, and of today. Life goes on, as it always does and must.

Last night, Steffen and I flew to Geneva, and as always, I'm thrilled to be home. Even with pouring rain, and an overwhelming feeling of sadness about the state of the United States (and the world, frankly), I'm still thrilled to be home.

We had a lovely drink with my sister Dania and laughed and talked about fun, silly, normal things. Today, I had several big work meetings in the city and talked about not-so-fun, less-silly, yet-still-totally-normal things. Tonight, I'm having dinner with my family, where we will undoubtedly be enjoying each other's company and talking about - yes - normal things.

So ... I guess in some ways there is a "new" normal on the horizon, and in other ways, things will stay as they always have been. I am still me, and I still have hopes and dreams and responsibilities, and so do all the wonderful people around me, and none of that changes. It can't. No one can take that away, no matter what.

And now if you'll excuse me, I have to go and get on with my normal evening.

Which involves introducing my new boyfriend to my Dad for the first time - and what could be more normal than that? ;-)

Love,

Joëlle

Side note: Far be it from me to get overly political, but the simple fact is that sometimes things do happen in the world around us that are definitely not the outcome we would have chosen. This can be really, really tough. And shocking. And sad.

And one of the best things we can do once the initial shock has passed is to hold on to the things that *haven't* actually changed. It's ok to still plan a fun night out with friends. It's ok to laugh at a silly joke. Or take a dance class. Or have a movie night at home. And it's definitely still ok to be yourself.

Yes, things change. And sometimes we do have to find a new normal. But where we can latch on to sentiments of normalcy and comfort and enjoyment and happiness, let's do so.

Because this too shall pass. And in the meantime, we can still be happy.

~~~~~

December 20th: Daydream When Necessary

This afternoon I was stuck in a three-hour group meeting at which there was no discernible purpose for me to attend.

Like, at all. It was on a subject that, at best, might impact my role in, say, six months. Until then, there's nothing I need to know on this topic. I even tried arguing beforehand that - given it's almost the end of the commercial year - perhaps spending the afternoon in said meeting wasn't the best use of my company time.

But nope, corporate bureaucracy dictated that everyone in the entire team had to be there, and indeed, there I sat. I said not one word during the entire session (and neither did anyone else at my level, so I pretty much rest my case).

Anyway, Happy Moments, yay! So at first, I was all scowly (on the inside, that is; hopefully, it wasn't too obvious on the outside). I was sitting at the table, mechanically "hmmm-ing" from time to time, and hammering Maltesers into my mouth like they were Valium tablets. Occasionally, I'd lean forward, pretending to scrutinize something on the videoconference screen, and then nodding slowly in what I hoped was a knowing fashion.

But at some point in that long, long meeting, I somehow transcended losing the will to live.

The solution? Daydreams! And while I think all of us regularly daydream at work, I went crazy with the daydreams today. I daydreamed about starting businesses, taking all sorts of trips, holding imaginary conversations with everyone from Steffen to my mom to Roger Federer, and generally just going to my various different happy places.

Now, I know that we all tend to spend approximately 99% of our time either caught up in the past or imagining the future, and that we should all

161

therefore try to spend more time in The Now. That's one of the key points behind meditation. But what about when The Now totally sucks?!? Shouldn't we all have a little safe, happy space we can escape to?

I think yes. And I certainly enjoyed my time running around that space today.

Love,

Joëlle

Side note: I'd recommend daydreaming to anyone as a solid last resort when you really don't want to deal with the current situation. It's obviously not appropriate for every situation, but if you're literally just sitting somewhere with nothing to contribute, then I'd argue it's a lot better to let your mind wander into Dreamworld than it would be to stew in angry silence.

And of course, ideally your daydreams would not only provide some escape, but also take you towards more productive ideas: if you're daydreaming because you're in a difficult work situation, for instance, can you daydream about alternate professional opportunities that might help ensure you don't have too many more days like this? If a relationship is getting you down, can you daydream about ways to make things better? If you're worried about finances, can you daydream about potential alternate sources of income?

Obviously, daydreams in themselves won't actually change anything. As it says in the introduction to this book, actions trump thoughts, intentions, and dreams. Actions are what actually create change.

But dreams can create that spark that eventually leads you down the path *to* change. Dreams can get you going and keep you hopeful.

And when all else fails, daydreams can get you through really, really boring meetings.

~~~~~

Tying Up Loose Ends

There will always be some Sad Days, of course. I mean, looking on the bright side, those sad days help us distinguish from the happier ones! So let's not shy away from them, and let's not pretend they're never going to happen again, just because we've made XYZ change in our lives. But there are still a couple of things I believe we can do about them:

First, let's not give them too much power. Acknowledge them, yes. Let them take over and totally ruin our day/week/moment, no. Don't allow any part of your brain to describe your day using superfluous terms of "worst day EVER!" in some sort of misguided ploy for self-sympathy. The objective here is to ultimately get over the sadness, not to replay and magnify the sadness over and over.

Second, let's make a distinction between days where something truly sad has happened and those moments when we're just feeling kind of blue. Again, it's ok to feel blue, but it's not ok to let our mind pretend that things are just AWFUL when nothing particularly bad has actually happened to evidence that.

Third, have a little reward to look forward to. If you're feeling upset at work, for instance, actually tell yourself what you're going to do as soon as you get out of work for the day. Maybe it's buy cupcakes. Maybe it's exercise. Maybe it's calling a friend to vent. Whatever works for you and can help you count down the seconds until you're there rather than here.

Fourth, if you KNOW you're going to have a Sad Day (returning from a vacation, for instance, or being roped into something you really don't want to be doing), see if you can prep a few mini-Happy Moments ahead of time. Pre-schedule some little breaks in your day when you'll be able to clear your head, call a friend, take a walk around the block, whatever. They're worth factoring into your day ahead of time, so that it can't all be bad.

Fifth, when all else fails, daydream. Just pretend this is not actually happening to you right now. It may be a bit of a cheap tactic, but sometimes we all just need a bit of an escape, so let's not pretend it can't help.

Sixth, come up with a mantra to repeat to yourself. Whatever version of "This too shall pass" works for YOU. Because it absolutely will, and you know it.

I hope these tips are helpful. They certainly worked for me during my year of Happy Moments, and they still work for me today whenever I have a Sad Day. And there are probably lots and lots of other things that you can do about your own Sad Days, so it's really all about finding whatever works for you. Have a plan of attack for when they strike! And be proud of yourself for doing so!

I do, of course, wish you very, very few Sad Days in your future. But for when they inevitably happen, I hope you'll know what to do, and I hope you won't take that sadness with you any farther than it needs to go.

This Too Shall Pass.

~~~~~

Prompt 9: What About When I Feel Sad?

This chapter's prompt is all about creating a personal plan of attack for when those Sad Days inevitably strike. It's about recognizing them for what they are, and knowing what you're going to do about them, with the ultimate goal of having fewer of them over time. And remember: having a sad day every once in a while, does not make you a sad person – it should help you recognize that overall, you're pretty happy!

What easily-obtained reward could I look forward to the next time I have a Sad Day? (e.g., cupcakes, a walk outside, taking a bath...) _____

_____

_____

What mini-breaks/escapes/rewards could I be ready to use if I know (or feel pretty sure) that I have a Sad Day coming up in the near future? (e.g., phone a friend, play a quick round of Angry Birds, go for coffee...)

_____

_____

Are there any places/people/patterns that I have noticed seem to go along with my feeling sad or experiencing Sad Days? If so, are there steps I could take to minimize those in my life? _____

_____

_____

Copy down the following phrase, or any similar mantra that speaks to YOU: This Too Shall Pass. "_____

_____

_____."

Chapter 10: Time to Create YOUR Happy Moments

Aka, the "We totally got this" chapter.

At last we're ready to talk about happiness creation. By now we've observed, we've noticed, we've enjoyed, we've remembered, and we've hopefully gotten to know ourselves better in terms of our own happiness. Time now, then, to take a more active role and work on really making those Happy Moments happen even more often.

From my experience, I'd say there are two parts to making this happen:

1) Finding ways to bring more unnecessary-but-fun activities or experiences into your life;

2) Showing gratitude for what comes to you out of the chances you take

Let's take these each in turn. First, the activities side of things. This is similar to Chapter 6 when we challenged ourselves, except here we're not necessarily talking about *big* challenges. It's not about straying far outside your usual comfort zone; it's more about caring enough to bring *small* changes into the activities we take on, or the new things we try, whether we do them regularly or just try them out once. The "unnecessary" side of this is important: this is something you're curious about, something outside the norms of any boxes that need to be checked or any commitments you've previously made. These little, fun activities should be possible answers to the question of "What COULD I do today?" rather than "What SHOULD I do today?"

Second, the gratitude. Simply taking a moment, here and there, to recognize the opportunities that come our way as a result of those small changes we're making. It's a time where you can let that little inner voice speak up with a "Hey, that was cool – thanks for that!" This doesn't mean that you have to love every little activity you take on, or that every chance you take will pay off in exactly the way you had hoped; it's more about recognizing that hey, you tried something, and that in itself was sort of cool.

I had lots and lots and LOTS of opportunities for gratitude during my year of Happy Moments, and I really hope that showed in how I talked about my experiences: whether it was something really small like trying out a coloring book, or something slightly more consequential like asking my cute, future-boyfriend out on a date, that "thank you" moment was important. It helped cement that I *was* making positive efforts and changes in my life, and helped me acknowledge those moments rather than simply letting them pass by.

Another way to think about gratitude is the concept of "Thank you, more please," an idea that comes from the movie *happythankyoumoreplease*. [10] The concept is, whenever something good happens to you, or whenever you feel happy, you take a little moment to send a quick message of gratitude to the Universe (or God, or whatever entity works for you) by saying those four little words:

Thank You, More Please.

This concept pretty much summed up everything I'd been trying to do with Those Happy Moments from the very beginning. I love its simplicity: notice what you're feeling, acknowledge it, put a little gratitude out into the world at large, and then simply ask for more of the same.

More happiness. Simple as that.

So again, the first step in this chapter is to *create* the opportunities, and the second step is to remember the "Yay, thank you!" feeling that we've hopefully been cultivating so far in this book through our noticing, acknowledging, enjoying, and remembering of Happy Moments.

I feel this is actually the most rewarding type of Happy Moments, regardless of whether or not they're as "exciting" as other kinds, such as going on adventures.

You're really making something happen for yourself here, and not because you need to, but just because you're consciously bringing a little extra spark into your life.

Here are a few examples I created:

~~~~~

January 26th: My New Toy

I got a new toy today. The Enchanted Forest coloring book by Johanna Basford.[11] As we likely all know by now, adult coloring has been experiencing a craze lately (at one point in 2015, 5 of the top 10 books on Amazon were coloring books for adults[12]). They're being used to relax, to improve focus and fine motor skills, and to aid with more restful sleep. They may even help with Alzheimer's by bringing back childhood memories.

Since I'm all about mindfulness and creativity in this new & improved 2016, I wanted in. Some people might think it's ridiculous for an adult woman to get excited about a coloring book. But to that I say: I'm a grown-up, and I can do whatever I want! (My mommy said so.)

I ordered it a few days ago, and it fortuitously arrived at my office today right before I needed to jump on a 3-hour conference call that demanded no active participation from me. I listened in with one ear, while turning leaves pink and jazzing up an owl. I loved it (the coloring). Keep talking, people!

Starting with the cover page on my first coloring adventure since, oh, about 1987, I had no idea what sort of time commitment I was getting myself into. It took me two-and-a-half hours to color that one page!

Extrapolating that, given that there are 84 pages in the book, I'm looking at about 210 hours of sheer entertainment and relaxation. That's the best £4.99 I've ever spent!

I know it's silly. And I'm completely ok with that.
Because I'm silly too.
Love,
Joëlle

Side note: I left that coloring book sitting on my desk the entire time I worked for that company. And while I rarely did have time to indulge in actual coloring at the office, the simple fact of seeing it there helped bring a little much-needed happiness during those dark moments when I struggled with how much I didn't like the job. I ended up surrounding the coloring book with pretty pictures of travels around the world, too, giving me easily the jazziest desk on the entire floor. Sometimes, small visual reminders of things that do make you happy can help trick your mind in those less-than-happy moments!

~~~~~

February 11ᵗʰ: Walk This Way

I took a different route on my walk to work this morning. I'm among the 10% or so of Londoners who are lucky enough to walk to their place of employment, and since getting here nearly seven months ago, I've always taken exactly the same path.

And after all, why wouldn't I? It's the shortest route, only taking me about 22 minutes.

But today, the sun was shining, the birds were singing, I didn't need to be in to the office that early...and so I thought, time for a change!

I felt like such a rebel, turning RIGHT when I exited my building. This was a whole new world opening up to me, just steps from my front door! Not five minutes away was a grassy, fenced-in square I'd never circled before. A tree was beautifully in bloom. There were pretty London row houses, and brand new shops I'd never known existed. Including one with the coolest name I've ever heard: Timorous Beasties.

I pressed my nose against the window, but couldn't discern what it was they might sell. "Open only by appointment," a sign on the door cryptically stated. It appeared to be some sort of fabric store.

I have to get in to Timorous Beasties.
I want a custom-made armchair, just so I can casually tell people, "Oh, that? It's Timorous Beasties."

Everything went right this morning as I meandered down these new streets. The weather was beautiful. People were smiling. A nice old lady wished me a cheerful "Good morning!" as we crossed paths. It took me a little longer to get to where I was going, but isn't that what makes life interesting sometimes?

I think so.

Love,

Joëlle

Side note: I ended up loving this route to work, and started leaving a little earlier most mornings in order to walk that way. It was quieter, less traveled, and had nicer sights than the shorter route did. Something I'd figured would just be a one-time whim turned into something regular and enjoyable, and every time I did take that route, I was so glad I'd discovered it! It helps me think about what other one-time things I could try that might end up being better than expected!

~~~~~

February 14th: Tomatoes Are Red, Violets Are Blue...

Well, it's Valentine's Day...again.

As many of us know, this isn't necessarily the most exciting day of the year when you're single. Most of the V-Days in my life have been spent solo, and I suppose as one gets older, one does start to wonder how much longer one will have before one dies alone in one's one-person apartment. (Note: When I say "one," I mean "me.")

But! This year, I resolved, SOMEONE was going to do something romantic for me! Someone was going to buy me FLOWERS!

(Second note: When I say "someone," I also mean "me." We're developing a theme here.)

So I put on a chic red sweater, got all gussied up, and headed to Marks & Spencer's. I know this isn't necessarily the sexiest place to buy flowers, but, well, I also needed groceries. One needs to cut a few corners when one is one's own Valentine.

Reaching the florist section of the store, I was vaguely thinking of buying myself some red roses. A classic for the occasion, after all.

And then...something caught both my eye and my imagination. What if, I thought, instead of buying myself roses - so perishable! So temporary! - I instead potted my own plant?

You have to understand that this is a pretty revolutionary idea for someone who has unintentionally killed pretty much every form of vegetation she's ever brought home. I swear I had a ficus commit suicide on me once, back in 2006. I've never recovered.

Long story short, I went in for red roses and came home with a tomato plant. A cherry tomato dwarf cascading maskotka, to be precise.

The instructions on the tin said "Simply sow and add water."

'I can sow!' I exclaimed to no one in particular. 'I can SO sow! I can sow SO hard!'

Once home, I realized there were additional instructions inside the tin. "Fill the tin with compost provided," I was told. "Scatter the seeds evenly on top and cover with a thin layer of the remaining compost."

Right away, this presented a bit of a poser: If I fill the tin with the 'compost provided,' shouldn't I by definition not have 'remaining' compost? Am I overthinking this?

Whatever, I thought. I pressed on. I filled. I scattered. I covered. I freakin' sowed.

My tinned-and-compost-covered seeds are now sitting on my kitchen windowsill, "in a bright position," as instructed. They should be blossoming into fruit by...

...July. I'll have tomatoes by July.

If I am dating someone by then, I will make him every tomato dish there is. I will make salads and soups and pasta sauce and homemade ketchup. I will make him a STEW.

Until then, we play the waiting game. Everything great is worth waiting for.

Happy Valentine's Day to all!

Love,

Joëlle

Side note: Yeah, I never got those tomatoes I was so enthusiastic about. On May 19th, I blogged about fighting a losing battle with dead leaves, and shortly thereafter, I had to jettison the entire plant. My green thumb let me down yet again.

But that's not the point! The point is that I didn't *need* to plant tomatoes, but I did anyway because it was something a little different that I thought might just brighten up my day. And it did! While the experiment ultimately failed in this particular case, I still had several months of watching my efforts gradually come to life on my windowsill. I still enjoyed thinking back on that one day I *sowed*. I still appreciated my positive attitude towards what could have simply been another depressingly-single Valentine's Day.

So again, don't discard the opportunity to try little new things. If, at worst, it doesn't work out, haven't you still tried something? Don't you still have a memory and a story to tell? Wasn't that – dare I say – kind of fun to experiment with? Go forth and try!

~~~~~

September 6th: Today's The Day

Ever had a random day that you've just been waiting seemingly FOREVER for? And then suddenly it's that day and it's today, and you're super duper excited, but also a little nervous because what if it's not all that after all?

And then you think, sod it, I'll just roll with things and see where they go, and then you think, really? and then you say "Really!" out loud, and ... pretty soon you realize you're having an absolutely ridiculous conversation with yourself and maybe you should just take a deep breath, relax your shoulders, and move on.

Anyway, today is that day, somewhat appropriately on the 250th day of the year, and it's finally here! And yes, I'm being intentionally cryptic!

So read between the lines if you will, and I'm just going to smile, shake off any nerves, and take things one day at a time.

(Yay!)

Love,

Joëlle

Side note: This was the night of my first date with my now-boyfriend Steffen, which had been a loooong time coming – I'd had a crush on him for longer than even he thinks! And since we lived in different countries, we'd been planning this date for something like two months. I couldn't believe it was finally there.

So showing gratitude here *before* the date even happened made me that much more excited for what I was certain would be a great thing. It was taking that unnecessary-but-fun chance of asking him out, and then recognizing how excited I was that it paid off, that made the anticipation and experience that much more special. Being grateful for opportunities definitely enhances experiences, so don't skimp on it!

Starting a great relationship wasn't a part of my original plan at the beginning of the year – it was the cherry on top. The more I tried new things and showed gratitude for the opportunities coming my way, the more opportunities *did* come my way. And that meant I was creating that much more happiness!

This may sound cheesy. But try it. Take a stab at something new. Get excited about it. Shrug your shoulders if it doesn't work out. And if it does, be thankful! And keep noticing what else might come your way as a result of taking those small chances.

Who knows? You might end up happier as a result.

~~~~~

November 19th: The Big 3-5

I'm currently sitting in a Lisbon hotel waiting for the clock to strike midnight and mark the start of my 35th birthday. Since birthdays are typically a day where you say thank you for gifts you receive, I just want to show a little gratitude today for a few of the more significant blessings I'll be taking with me on my new journey around the sun.

And since I'm now midway through my fourth decade, I thought I'd narrow this down to the three (and-a-half) things I'm most grateful for that have come my way in the past year.

1) I'm really grateful for my boyfriend Steffen. Yes, I know that's schmaltzy, and I never thought I'd be one of those girls. But I also never thought I'd have the opportunity to be one of those girls! I spent my entire twenties really, really, depressingly single. Then from ages 30-33, I was in an unhealthy on-and-off relationship. Then I got dumped, moved to London, and was single again for over a year. I honestly thought it would never happen for me. So what I'm saying is, it is possible to meet someone who is kind, who makes you laugh, who challenges you, and who makes you feel good about yourself ... even if you're well into your thirties (or beyond!) "It's supposed to be easy," I kept telling myself whenever I imagined what a good relationship would look like. And as I found out this year - when you get it right - it really IS easy!

2) I'm really grateful for my experience training as a yoga teacher. I've blogged about this a lot this year, and yeah, I'm disappointed that I've barely taught since then, but the feeling of awe is real. I've never enjoyed learning about anything this much before. It brought a lot of emotions to the surface, helped me continue to get to know myself better, and gave me hope and clues that just maybe, there's something out there for me.

3) I'm really grateful for this blog. I'm grateful that I've stuck it out, and that it proves to me I am someone who can get things done, and who can be motivated and creative. I've found importance in something that virtually no one else even knows about, I've put a little piece of myself into all 324 entries thus far, and damn it, I'm a writer. Not a published one, nor a successful one, nor even necessarily a good one. But I write because it means something to me, and this blog is my proof. Happy Moments, warts and all.

3.5) I'm continuously grateful for this life, even when it frustrates, angers, or saddens me. The fact that I even have Happy Moments to write about - that I have a terrific family, crazy-wonderful friends, a roof over my head, money coming in, opportunities, and even scary unknowns is pretty wonderful. Call me a walking cliché, but there you have it. I don't say thank you enough for all that, so here it goes: Thank. You.

And with that, let's get this party started!

Love,

Joëlle, 35 and still growing

Side note: I said that these things had "come my way" in the past year, but if I'm honest, I think that phrasing did me a disservice. These were things that *I* brought into my life, and that *I* consciously created.

And these things started out as small! When I asked my boyfriend out on a date, I wasn't trying to form a fabulously perfect relationship right off the bat – I just thought he was cute and wanted to get to know him! (And by the way, he tells the story differently.) When I signed up for my yoga teacher training, I didn't think it'd be the earth-shattering experience it ended up being – I just wanted to learn more about yoga! And when I wrote my first blog entry, I *definitely* didn't think I'd write every day or that it would become what it did – I just kind of wanted to write something!

But those "small" efforts, those risks of trying something just a little bit different gradually led to BIG changes in my life. You really just never know where a small effort might take you – and there's only one way to find out!

~~~~~

Tying Up Loose Ends

Going beyond whatever randomly comes our way and actually creating additional happiness in our lives on a regular basis can make a huge difference. Creating happy opportunities and trying new activities doesn't have to be as challenging as it may feel, and it actually gets a lot easier with time. All it really requires is an open mind, a little curiosity, and the willingness to answer the question: "What COULD I do today?"

My single best tip around finding and pursuing unnecessary-but-fun activities is this: Just do it. Honestly. If you come across something intriguing, or have a new idea about something interesting, and maybe you're kind of on the fence about whether to try it, or it seems silly or pointless ... just do it. There will always be an excuse *not* to do something, but chances are, there's a reason this caught your eye. Honor that, and instead of spending time and energy worrying about whether you should try it, just do it! And again, we're not talking about huge, expensive, time-consuming activities here. Maybe it's taking a different route to work (walking, driving, taking a different bus line, etc.) Maybe it's a new type of cuisine you've never tried before. Maybe it's joining a book club, or going to a community event, or talking to someone you've never talked to before. Just try it! And if you don't like it, you never have to do it again. And if you *do* like it, believe me, you'll be glad you went ahead and just did it.

Also, think about coming up with some sort of personal gratitude mantra. It can be "Thank you, more please" or anything that works for you. It could also be as simple as a mental fist pump, just as long as you take the time to include it. Gratitude helps us recognize the efforts we make and the results that come out of them.

Having consciously created a whole bunch of Happy Moments in 2016, I'm happy to say I'm still constantly on the lookout for creating more of them a year later. The more I create small bursts of happiness, the more likely big ones are to come along, and the happier I feel overall. And isn't that really the point?

I think so. And I think it can work for you too.

~~~~~

Prompt 10: Time to Create YOUR Happy Moments

This final prompt is about really exercising that creative muscle when it comes to making more Happy Moments happen. We've all got this creative muscle, by the way – sometimes it just takes a little flexing! The great news is that after working your way through the first nine chapter prompts, you've hopefully got a better sense of what happiness means to you, why you're interested in bringing more happiness into your life, how to tackle challenges and create a plan of attack for Sad Days, how to form happier habits, and just generally more about being yourself. So you've totally got this!

What unnecessary-but-fun activities COULD you do today? Or tomorrow? Or next week? (Hint: there is no "right" answer here – just start scribbling down whatever comes to mind!) _____

_____

_____

Which of the above activities WILL you do this week? (Hint: No need to go overboard here. Just pick one – but really commit that you will try it this week. It doesn't have to be scary, expensive, or time-consuming!)

_____

_____

Are you proud of yourself for making efforts to create additional happiness in your life? (The answer *should* be yes; and if it isn't, why not?) _____

_____

_____

Write down a gratitude mantra that works for you and that you can incorporate into your overall attitude (if you can't think of one, write down "Thank you, more please!") _____

_____

_____

Conclusion: What's the Payoff?

We've now worked our way through 10 chapters of happiness. Ways to bring more of it into our daily lives, what to do when facing adversity or sadness, how to challenge ourselves, and how to simply notice random moments that might bring us a little more joy.

With that said, I do hope this hasn't actually felt too much like work. Because happiness is something that is already all around us, not to mention within us as well. If you can just sensitize yourself as to where to look for it, you'll find it was there already, just waiting for you to notice it.

For me, my year of Happy Moments changed the way I thought about my own life. What had been a "good-ish" life before, became one with a lot more excitement, confidence, and – of course – happiness. I liked who I was as a person a lot more than before. I believed in myself a lot more. I gave myself so much more to be grateful for, and I had so much more to look forward to in the future.

And since then, the really exciting thing is that these feelings have stuck with me. Again, it's all about exercising the happiness muscle to start doing more work for you! Even a year after ending my blogging experiment, I'm still noticing the random moments, keeping up with the positive habits I'd formed, and creating more happy memories every single day. It's helped me make big changes in my outside life, too: quitting the corporate job I'd never liked, moving to Germany to live with Steffen, finally writing my first book, and so much more. I don't think I'd be where I am today if I hadn't banged out that first blog entry on January 1st, 2016, without even knowing what I was doing at the time.

And so I encourage anyone to look for ways to find and create a little additional happiness in their own lives. Even if it feels cheesy, or silly, or even pointless at times – isn't the trade-off still worth it, for an even slightly-happier life?

Think about it: What are YOUR dreams? What do you wish you could accomplish, big or small? What have you ever thought, "Huh, that could be fun" about? Now ask yourself, why didn't you try that thing? Why are your dreams still dreams? What could you do to make them a reality?

I truly hope you'll pursue something new, exciting, and happy after reading this book. No matter what it might be.

And I hope you find lots of Happy Moments along the way.

Love,

Joëlle

P.S. Here was my final blog entry:

~~~~~

January 1st, 2017: 366 Days Gone By

And just like that, it's 2017.

2016 has ended, and with it, so has my little one-year blog project. Which I never even intended to be a one-year blog project. It just sort of ... happened.

And I think that's how a lot of things that end up being really personally important and special start out, when you think about it. Start with a vague idea, mix in a little spontaneity, stay committed and stubborn, and ... surprise yourself.

*This blog never "became" much. I didn't make a dime off it, or garner that many likes, or ever even - *grumble, grumble* - look into setting up a mailing list. But it still mattered to me. It mattered enough for me to leave parties early, to snitch 15 minutes from other more "important" activities if necessary, and - most importantly - to keep my eyes constantly open for a little*

Happy Moment to write about that day. It somehow became my thing this past year, when I didn't even know I was looking for a thing. And every so often, a comment from a friend, like, "Joëlle, I love your blog!" was enough to absolutely make my day.

I'll be honest: I'm still scared about 2017. I have a few plans that scare me, and that I sometimes think are flat-out stupid and risky. They feel hard. They feel uncertain. I was struggling with my planner earlier today, and I just don't know if I'm going to be able to do it. But it helps to know that we DO do things we aren't certain about, all the time. This blog is proof of it. And, you guys: Happy Moments are everywhere.

This won't be the end of my writing. I really do want to turn some of these entries into short stories. I'd like for there to be a book. I'd even like to keep blogging, albeit not every day. I really must figure out how to set up a mailing list. So please, don't hesitate to check in again.

And now, to end the Happy Moments blog - at least in its original incarnation - I want to close with a huge, huge thank you to YOU. Whether you read one entry, or all of them. Whether you regularly left a comment, or simply sent a little positive thought my way. Whether we're already friends, or you stumbled onto here somehow through the magic of the Internet.

Thank you, for all of it. I am sitting here, inspired and happy, and I couldn't have done it alone.

I hope you too will take many Happy Moments with you from this past year, and kick off the next one to be the best year yet.

With much, much love,

Joëlle

~~~~~

Cheat Sheet: Top Ten Tips for More Happy Moments

Quick hints distilling the essence of each chapter – in only one or two sentences! Keep these in mind and see which ones work best for you to bring more Happy Moments into YOUR life.

1) Stop listening to the negative, cruel "WTF" voices and doubts in your head that may tell you what you're doing isn't worthwhile. It is. Keep going.

2) Notice your own personal quirks to get to know yourself better. This will help prove to you that you can find reasons *every single day* to smile.

3) Keep some perspective when adverse setbacks strike. These experiences do not define your life or who you are.

4) Celebrate your friends, and flash back to the fun times you've had together. The more you take away from this, the better a friend you can be to yourself.

5) Seek out adventures in your everyday life to help you go beyond your comfort zone.

6) Challenge yourself by jumping off that cliff. Because at some point, a net of some kind *will* catch you. You *can* do this.

7) To form better, happier habits, take daily baby steps, stay focused, and forgive yourself for not doing this sooner.

8) Stay curious and notice the random things happening around you. They can be an endless source of happiness to counteract mundaneness and negativity.

9) If you feel sad, acknowledge that, schedule rewards for yourself, and if all else fails, use daydreams to escape. This too shall pass.

10) To create more happiness, find ways to bring more unnecessary-but-fun activities into your life, and be grateful for what comes of them.

Love,
Joëlle

Acknowledgments

It turns out you can't write a book about happiness without recognizing how incredibly lucky you are to be well-surrounded! I would especially like to thank:

My wonderful friend Jeanne Feldkamp, without whose encouragement this book would not exist.

My sister Dania, for her proofreading prowess and for just generally being the best little sister in the world.

My parents Debi and Jean-Maurice and my brother Tiago for their constant support.

Miguel Mayher, Tottie Yomoka, and the rest of the Morning Maker crew.

Laura Penwell, whose cover design brought this book to life, and Joanna Kolan, whose patience in trying to get a good photo of me knew no bounds!

My oldest and dearest friend Anna Lundstrom, who somehow always managed to read my blog entries within 30 seconds after I'd uploaded them.

Lori and Nichole Blackburn, whose creative and positive spirits have inspired many of my own pursuits.

Everyone who followed *Those Happy Moments* in its original blog form, especially my most faithful readers: Anamika, Anna, Betty, Claudia, Dania, Debi, Francisca, Ketan, Liz, Meredith, and Ritesh.

To cover my bases, everyone I have ever met in my entire life.

And lastly, I would like to thank Steffen, for making every moment happier than the last.

Love,
Joëlle

Endnotes

[1] Pham, Cammi. "You Will Always Suck At What You Do, Until You Do This." *cammiphan,* http://www.cammipham.com/will-always-suck/. Accessed 18 February 2016.

[2] Sharma, Robin (@RobinSharma). "Don't live the same year 75 times and call it a life." 30 March 2014, 5:00 a.m. Tweet.

[3] West, Kanye. "Stronger." 2007. *Graduation*. MP3.

[4] Diamond, Dan. "Just 8% of People Achieve Their New Year's Resolutions. Here's How They Do It." *Forbes*. https://www.forbes.com/sites/dandiamond/2013/01/01/just-8-of-people-achieve-their-new-years-resolutions-heres-how-they-did-it/#1e48ab21596b. Accessed 2 July 2016.

[5] Kinsella, Sophie. *Finding Audrey*. New York: Delacorte Press, 2015. Print.

[6] Wikipedia contributors. "F. F. E. Yeo-Thomas." *Wikipedia, The Free Encyclopedia*. Accessed 12 February 2016.

[7] Copping, Jasper. "Historian Reveals the Second World War Hero who Inspired the Creation of James Bond." *The Telegraph*. http://www.telegraph.co.uk/culture/film/jamesbond/9560403/Historian-reveals-the-Second-World-War-hero-who-inspired-the-creation-of-James-Bond.html. Accessed 12 February 2016.

[8] Firth, Niall. "First Blue Plaque for British Spy as WWII Secret Agent who Survived Gestapo is Honoured." *Daily Mail*. http://www.dailymail.co.uk/news/article-1262551/Famous-British-WWII-spy-The-White-Rabbit-survived-Gestapo-torture-honoured-blue-plaque.html. Accessed 12 February 2016.

[9] Shine Communications PR Agency, London EC1R 4RB. http://www.shinecom.com/about.

[10] *Happythankyoumoreplease*. Directed by Josh Radnor, Anchor Bay Films, 2010.

[11] Basford, Johanna. *Enchanted Forest: An Inky Quest and Colouring Book.* London: Laurence King Publishing Ltd, 2015. Print.

[12] Halliwell, Rachel. "Hooked on Colouring In! Why ARE Thousands of Grown Women Suddenly Reaching for Their Crayons?" *Daily Mail.* http://www.dailymail.co.uk/femail/article-3135291/Hooked-colouring-s-peculiar-craze-thousands-grown-women-suddenly-ready-Crayons.html. Accessed 26 January 2016.

77611404R00114

Made in the USA
Lexington, KY
29 December 2017